Conversatio

Conversations on a Train

Regina Ryan

Australian eBook Publisher

Conversations on a Train by Regina Ryan
Published by Australian eBook Publisher
www.AustralianEbookPublisher.com.au
© Regina Ryan

1st Edition 2016, pbk.
ISBN: 978-1-925516-40-1
Designer: Sharnai James-McGovern, Australian eBook Publisher

National Library of Australia Cataloguing-in-Publication entry:
Creator: Ryan, Regina, author.
Title: Conversations on a train / Regina Ryan.
ISBN: 9781925516401 (paperback)
          9781925516395 (ebook : mobi)
          9781925516388 (ebook : epub)
Subjects: Ryan, Regina.
          Ryan, Regina--Childhood and youth.
          Bulgarians--Australia--Biography.
          Immigrants--Australia--Biography.
          Bulgaria--Social life and customs.
          Australia--Social life and customs.

Also available as an ebook from major ebook vendors.

Contents

Chapter One: Bulgarian pride 7

Chapter Two: Snapshots of my Bulgarian childhood 14

Chapter Three: The big move to Australia 24

Chapter Four: First waves of culture shock and the
                    Australian schooling system 28

Chapter Five: A 15-year-old Bulgarian's preconceived ideas
                    about life in Australia 36

Chapter Six: The child and the state—Bulgarian style
                    parenting and school 39

Chapter Seven: Bulgarian art, the royal connection and
                    a visit to the mausoleum 58

Chapter Eight: Bulgarian music 70

Chapter Nine: Bulgarian Film and TV 78

Chapter Ten: Bulgarian humour, anecdotes, fairy tales
                    and adult literature 84

Chapter Eleven: Return to Bulgaria and the beginning of
                    Australian university life 102

Chapter Twelve: Misunderstandings and little-known
                    facts about socialist Bulgaria 126

Chapter Thirteen: The many layers of homesickness 150

Chapter Fourteen: A taste of Bulgarian food greatness 163

Chapter Fifteen: What Bulgaria has given the world 178

Appendix 189

Acknowledgments 195

CHAPTER ONE

Bulgarian pride

E lias Canetti, the great Bulgarian novelist and nonfiction writer and winner of the 1981 Nobel Prize in Literature, once said, 'Anything I subsequently experienced had already happened in Rousse.' Born in Rousse, Bulgaria in 1905 to a family of wealthy merchants, he spent his childhood in Bulgaria ('Rousse, where I came into the world, was a marvellous city for a child'), and the rest of his life in Britain, Germany, Austria and Switzerland. He held Bulgarian, British and Swiss citizenships, and spoke Bulgarian, German, English, French and Ladino.

I find this quote fascinating given his cosmopolitan, multicultural background, and even more so because my personal experience outside of Bulgaria, in Australia to be more precise, has been the opposite. Nothing of my life in Bulgaria prepared me for life in Australia.

My moves between Bulgaria and Australia took place in a different era altogether—the early 1990s—and between a country of ancient civilisations, socialist realism statues and European boulevards, and a country of white picket fences, skyscrapers and red earth bush.

My personal feelings about Bulgaria are more accurately captured by another Bulgarian, the author and journalist Stefan Gruev. Gruev (1922–2006) was a political emigrant who spent 46 of his 83 years away from his native country, mostly in Switzerland, France and the United States of America, where he was the head of Paris Match magazine for 20 years. He is known to me through his book, *Crown of Thorns*, which is about Boris III, the last Bulgarian Tsar.

At the beginning of the book he describes for foreigners how Bulgarians feel about their country. 'It may sound exceedingly sentimental to foreigners when Bulgarians talk about their love for their country. Who doesn't love their country? But to a Bulgarian this attachment means a lot more. This feeling they have for their country is so passionate it can only be compared to the state of a person in love—all consuming, romantic, exalted, jealous love.' Stefan Gruev attributes this grand love Bulgarians have for their country partly to the natural beauty of the country, the mountains, the Rose Valley; the only one of its kind in the world, the beauty of the coast, the smell of Bulgarian flowers, the sky, which 'has a particular colour' in Bulgaria, and even the water, which Bulgarians are convinced 'tastes different'. He does admit that his perspective on Bulgaria and that of Bulgarians he knows is without a doubt romantic and 'a little subjective' but he goes on to say: 'But perhaps this country really is exceptional or at the very least different from other countries.' I like people who romanticise their country to such a degree, particularly if that country happens to be Bulgaria. I am one of those people.

You are by now wondering exactly what kind of a journey did you sign up for and what kind of conversations will we have? My objective is to reveal to you a great old country where Proto-Bulgarians, Thracians and Slavs were joined to become one ethnic whole, Bulgarian, a great medieval empire bordering on three seas, a kingdom, a people's republic, a so-called modern democracy and yes, Bulgaria has been, at one time or another, all of the above.

It's a great country that gave the world the Cyrillic alphabet (used in more than 50 different languages, including Russian), the Proto-Bulgarian calendar (the world's oldest and most accurate calendar in the world, as declared by UNESCO), and the world's oldest golden treasure (dating back to 4600 BC–4200 BC). This ancient country gave the world John Atanasoff, the inventor of the first electronic digital computer, the Atanasoff-Berry computer, and Petar Petrov, the NASA scientist and inventor of the world's first digital watch and the world's first wireless heart monitor.

Of course, these are all facts you can find in many history books, and I will make sure you encounter these facts again, in more detail, further along our journey, towards the end of the train line, when hopefully the likelihood of you memorising them will be greater.

What I hope to reveal to you most of all is the Bulgarian way of life, the Bulgarian psyche, and the way a Bulgarian relates to the world around in a light-hearted manner that will make you fall in love with all things Bulgarian. Since history books alone will not achieve that, I will attempt to present you with a little glimpse of the Bulgarian way through the story of my own Bulgarian life and most of all through stories and snapshots of my childhood.

Why, you may ask? Ordinarily, the reader has the task of figuring that out for themselves. Not so with this account. I am not a novelist or a writer and I therefore conclude that I do not have to comply with any of the rules, written or unwritten, that writers feel compelled to follow. At university I studied psychology for a decade, not literature, political science or economics, and my interests are primarily focused on the human experience; the thoughts and feelings of people, not creating characters and carefully developed storylines, and not the economic merits of various ideologies.

I only mention my background in psychology so that (hint, hint) you will immediately realise that I like listening and talking; often talking more than listening. This will be a spontaneous discourse, much like a conversation. However, the rigid rules required in the writing of a couple of theses has resulted in a strong propensity to prematurely announce my objectives before the build-up of any suspense or confusion sets in.

Having said that, I feel an obligation to point out that the experience of writing a doctoral dissertation has dulled my brain and created a great need within me to write something, or anything, without the limitations and rigid requirements of academic writing. I am going to rebel against all dry, academic writing requirements that have been imposed on me for a decade and therefore, you should expect this to be a subjective, spontaneous, sentimental and most of all highly romantic account (and not only should you expect this, but you should also feel I am fully justified in doing so).

But then, this is what Bulgaria does to you and this, by the way, is another Bulgarian tendency—to rebel against authority. Ferdinand of Saxe-Coburg and Gotha, second last Tsar of Bulgaria (and as the name suggests not remotely of Bulgarian blood, but more about him later) wrote to his son, Tsar Boris III, 'The Bulgarian, from the most simple to the most educated, every single one of them, are rebels and they have no respect for the crown.' This quote gives me a feeling of immense satisfaction, although I am not entirely against this institution. To this day, with all the shifts and sudden turns of our national fate and consequently our history, long as it may be, Bulgaria being one of the oldest countries in Europe, the two most revered Bulgarian national heroes are revolutionaries and exactly what Tsar Ferdinand would call ultimate rebels, Vasil Levski and Hristo Botev.

Vasil Levski is Bulgaria's most beloved national hero and greatest revolutionary, not only for strategising a nationwide revolutionary movement to liberate Bulgaria from the Ottoman Empire, but also for looking beyond Bulgaria's liberation and seeing a 'holy and pure republic' with ethnic and religious equality for all. Levski said, 'If I win—I win for all our people, if I lose—I lose only myself' and indeed, he was ultimately captured and executed by hanging on 19 February 1873. On that very spot, in the centre of Sofia, now stands a magnificent statue, which is annually covered by a sea of flowers.

All Bulgarians have a favourite Levski quote and mine is, 'Time is in us and we are in time. It changes us and we change it.' Levski's contemporary, and our second most beloved national hero, Hristo Botev, was a brilliant poet as well as a revolutionary, and he and Levski shared a home for a time—an abandoned mill in Romania.

He died in battle at the tender age of 27, three years after Levski, in 1876, but not before leaving some profound poems, one of which is dedicated to Levski's death, *The Hanging of Vasil Levski*, in which he writes, ' Weep on, weep on! Near Sofia town, A ghastly gallows I have seen standing, And your own son, Bulgaria, There with dreadful force is hanging.' That particular line, 'And your own son, Bulgaria' oh, how it always gets the Bulgarian blood pumping.

Levski and Botev are our most worthy heroes of recent times, but with a history dating back thousands of years, my Bulgarian pride leads me to mention a few of our ancient rulers so as to arouse your interest in our ancient history and lead you to discover the great deeds of Khan Asparuh (the son of Khan Kubrat, ruler of Old Great Bulgaria and founder of what is now known as Bulgaria in 681), Khan Tervel (he was called the Saviour of Europe for his decisive attack against the Arabs in the siege of Constantinople), Khan Krum (who introduced the first written laws in Bulgaria between 803–814), Tsar Boris I (who Christianised Bulgaria in the ninth century), and Tsar Simeon I (son of Boris I, who achieved not only the greatest expansion of our territory, bordering on three seas, but his reign between ninth and 10th century was also known as the Golden Age of Bulgarian culture).

In between some of these rulers there were a number of others but an unfortunate number of them seem to have been murdered by their cousins; one simply fled to Constantinople with the treasury and in the end Tsar Ivan Shishman managed to maintain Bulgaria as a major cultural centre but could not prevent the fall of the country to Ottoman rule in the 14th century. But enough of the history lesson.

Before you start to sense that I am aiming to Bulgarianise you, which would not be a false assumption, let me illustrate for you what the experience of reading this account will feel like to you. It will feel like meeting a stranger at a train station, who you find will be sitting next to you for several hours on your journey, and who, you quickly learn, is very talkative, especially about her love of her country, about which she feels a strong obligation to educate others.

You will start by saying, Bulgaria, 'Where is that?' or 'Oh, isn't that a former communist country? Were you part of the Soviet Union?' This will make my blood boil, but remembering that I have you sitting next to me on a moving train, unable to escape, my good-natured, friendly self will tell you that Bulgaria has a history of over 1330 years (if you include the several other great ancient civilisations that thrived on our land before we made it our own, a 7000 year history), and during that time yes, it was a socialist country for 44 years.

I am a child of the 1980s, therefore my childhood falls neatly right near the end of those socialist years, so you see socialism, as much as it is part of our history, and therefore part of our self-definition, it is still, in the grand scheme of Bulgarian things, only a small part of what Bulgaria was, or is. Bulgaria is infinitely greater than its socialist past and its socialist past is not at all what you may think.

But fear not, because by the time you get off the train and say your goodbyes, you will want to exchange phone numbers and email addresses because you will be so intrigued by Bulgaria, and what it means to be Bulgarian, you will stand at that platform, wondering how it is you never knew these things. You will go on your way, wondering if perhaps maybe somewhere down the line you have some Bulgarian relatives, you will be eager to listen to Bulgarian music, eat Bulgarian food, read Bulgarian books, watch Bulgarian films and most of all, visit this great country, walk the Bulgarian mountains, lie on the beach somewhere on the Black Sea, see the world's oldest golden treasure, enter ancient tombs and even see examples of socialist realism architecture.

I have already anticipated your excitement and I intend to cover all of the above-noted aspects of Bulgarianness. You will even be able to make yourself some Bulgarian food to complete your immersion in Bulgarian culture, not to mention significantly improve your health. And when you just wish you were there and when you wish you could get a glimpse of what it used to be like, I have just the right resources which will take you on a photographic journey of Bulgaria through the ages, everything from random people's personal photos to official advertising material.

Yes, it really is true what the Welsh writer Jan Morris wrote about Bulgarians after travelling around Bulgaria in 1990, 'No patriot on earth is more patriotic than a Bulgar'. So how is it, you may ask, that such a proud Bulgarian is living most of the year in Australia, of all places? Well, you keep your seat next to me and you shall find out. It is not a short story, but then again none of my stories are ever short.

CHAPTER TWO

Snapshots of my Bulgarian childhood

L et us begin this romantic, and sentimental tour of my Bulgarian childhood. I should point out that this story will contain a multitude of ironies. For example, the fact that I am writing this story, my personal account, is ironic, because I am a private person by nature and by upbringing. I was brought up to think that it is vulgar to begin too many sentences with 'I', to talk too much about yourself, and yet here I am screaming out loud superlatives to complete strangers, such as the reader, about my childhood and my life in Bulgaria. The only explanation I have as a way of reconciling this irony is that the simple and pure pride of being Bulgarian seems to be a part of the Bulgarian DNA. It is deeply encoded into our very soul.

Consider Atanas Burov, Bulgaria's wealthiest banker and a prominent politician of the 20th century, and how he ranked his life's loves and priorities at a time when he seems to have been disillusioned with the direction the country had taken. First, his mother; second, the motherland; third, his father and brother; and fourth, the honest Bulgarian patriots. Even a banker in Bulgaria ranks his motherland up there, second only to his mother.

Sure, that was a long time ago, and Bulgarian bankers of today are no longer made that way (not to mention that Bulgaria is not exactly known for its bankers) but we had one and I am sticking with him. He is also quoted as making this declaration: 'In 1922–

1923 I was in France in their most beautiful resort, Vichy. I had money and I had gold. I had deposits in foreign banks, but I was lonely, subdued and sad. Nothing can replace the motherland. She is your mother, she is your strength, she is everything.' These words take on a greater significance when you consider his personal story.

Born into one of Bulgaria's wealthiest banking families in 1875, when Bulgaria was still officially part of the Ottoman Empire, Burov had every advantage imaginable in life. His father spent 10 years training him to manage the family banks, after extensive study across Europe; law at the Sorbonne in Paris, political science and finance in Switzerland and London. At Oxford, he was so impressed with the study of psychology of trade, the masses and diplomacy, that years later, when he opened a university in Bulgaria, he included a similar course. When communism emerged as the dominant power Burov was offered several opportunities to leave the country. This old-school, cosmopolitan individual refused and insisted on living among his fellow Bulgarians.

Even when subjected to hardship, having had most of his personal assets and wealth confiscated, having been put under house arrest and later, issued a prison sentence by the ruling communists, he was writing that 'a person without a motherland, is a complete orphan' and declaring his love for Bulgaria. He subsequently died a sad death, his patriotism largely unappreciated by his countrymen for many years after his death, but that's another life lesson for us and beside the point (the point being that this country has a great many patriots) and I won't let it get in the way of my story.

Now let us take a romantic walk through my Bulgaria. Idyllic images pop up instantly, competing with each other for which memory should be told first. My childhood summers were filled with daily walks around the Sea Gardens in Burgas near my maternal grandparents' home, where sculptures pop up all around big garden beds of colourful flowers. My friends, the neighbours' children and I would walk past the open air theatre overlooking the Black Sea, take the beautiful steps leading down to the shore and walk on the famous Burgas jetty, discussing whatever life problems we happened to be encountering at that time.

I have countless memories of walking back home past the little restaurants and cafés overlooking the sea in the Sea Gardens, down Bogoridi Street, leading to the centre of the city exactly where my grandparents live. Sometimes there would be a folk festival and we would watch the colourful national costumes and vibrant dances. But any day of the week we would encounter grandmothers sitting out the front of houses and apartment block gardens gossiping, young mums in floral dresses with their strollers passing by, and gypsy ladies sweeping the streets. To this day when I see pink roses growing over dark green metal gates, I think of summer afternoon walks in Burgas.

My childhood friends and I would roam the streets from afternoon until dinnertime, spending our pocket money in corner shops, eating feta cheese pastry called *banichka*, drinking the acidic sweet fermented wheat drink called *boza*, and buying packets of roasted sunflower seeds from old ladies on the street. We would hang around the opera house, near my grandparents', and eat ice creams while overhearing opera rehearsals. We would play cards and spin the bottle, listen to Guns and Roses and Metallica, Roxette and Sinead O'Connor on a bench on someone's stereo, then rush home to watch a favourite TV show, the Spanish series *Blue Summer*. Then in the late afternoon we would venture out again, play badminton on the street, and dodge the odd bucket of cold water being thrown at us from nearby balconies by a grumpy grandmother annoyed with our noise.

When I finally made it home, I would find my grandma cooking in the kitchen and my great-grandma cooking on the kitchen balcony, while my grandfather would have been sent to the shops. My cousin, three years younger than me, would still be outside with the boys from our street, doing whatever it is boys do, building spaceships, jumping off any high surface and fighting with water guns, while I read a book on the living room balcony, stopping to gaze at the red and pink geranium my grandma kept on the balcony in ceramic dark green pots. I would take little breaks from reading and visit the kitchen, as much for the snacks as for the adult conversations, particularly if my aunty happened to be back from work. In the kitchen the most common sight would be that of tomatoes, peaches, apricots, cherries, cucumbers, mint, parsley, watermelon; all my summer favourites. But my afternoon snack was usually capsicum stuffed with feta cheese.

Dinnertime in summer was usually an affair involving four generations of the family, loud talking, a lot of gesturing, debates, watching the news, followed by some Bulgarian TV series and movies, comedy shows and then the late night TV concerts with popular music, during which, it was not unusual for people to get up and start spontaneously dancing around the living room.

Some nights my cousin and I would perform a play for the family, complete with music and the reciting of poems, all chosen by me, after many hours of forcing my cousin into highly reluctant yet sufficiently obedient learning of my chosen dialogue for him. My favourite time, however, was late at night, when everyone had gone to sleep and my great-grandmother would be up enjoying the silence of the night and her favourite relaxation hobby, embroidering, while telling stories of the past and all the characters that made up her youth and her life in the early 1900s.

Summer weekends were spent driving around in search of remote beaches on the Black Sea coast with aunties, uncles and cousins, and encountering medieval churches in one of Europe's oldest towns, Nessebar. Sometimes I would go to the central beach near our house with my grandfather, who would teach me the multiplication table while sitting in the sand. There were long afternoon naps, more book reading, more talking. Then there were trips to my grandparents' weekend house, Villa Regina; my cousin may tell you that I am the only one who calls it that, not true, just read the giant gates—Villa Regina. The house is a short drive from the centre of town, near a forest, and although as a little girl I was terrified of most living creatures, including crickets and butterflies, I loved eating cherries under the cherry tree.

Invariably, after spending most of June, July and August with my grandparents, the summer holidays would end and that would mean my return to Sofia for the beginning of the school year. I remember very well the first day of school, the 15th September, when wearing the school uniform, a white shirt with a navy blue pleated skirt, I along with my classmates would present our teachers with endless bunches of flowers.

In spite the fact that summer was my favourite time of year I also loved the changing of the seasons, and the green, red and yellow leaves covering the streets of Sofia. I remember catching trams and trolley buses with friends to go roller-skating outside the National Palace of Culture, or to walk around Sofia's *Borisova Gradina* (or Freedom Park, as it was known in socialist times). I remember the sight of young and old men playing chess in front of Ivan Vazov National Theatre in Sofia.

Images of women young and old walking, or rather, rushing through the streets of the centre of Sofia, always elegantly dressed, always in high heels, are fresh in my mind to this day. I remember visiting the open book markets and then spending the afternoons reading fairy tales and classics from around the world instead of doing my homework. I remember the embarrassment of having to wear woollen 'pipit' (houndstooth) pants instead of the corduroy all my friends were allowed to wear and rebelling by secretly putting on brown lipstick and lip liner at school.

Then there were the national days of celebration and the school outings organised to deliver flowers to various famous statues around the city. To this day, what defines Sofian architecture to me is the unique mixture of Soviet statues in public parks, metres away from yellow cobblestone streets and medieval sites next to buildings as varied as Stalinist Gothic (yes, it does exist, the former communist party headquarters) and Neo-Baroque (Sofia

University), and every other neo, Neo-Rococo, Neo-Renaissance, Neoclassicism.

Then there were the famous concrete tower blocks, *panelki*, plain and tidy when I was a child, with communal playgrounds for the many children frequenting them daily. I remember games with elastic involving intricate jumping procedures to avoid getting tangled up in the elastic, and badminton (minus the net), and dodge ball, or *narodna* as we call it.

I remember the tonnes of homework and I remember not doing my homework, and occasionally skipping class. I most definitely remember my parents' punishment—ice cold stares accompanied by some mild yelling, followed by the issuing of near eternal grounding orders. But I also remember regular family weekends exploring and picnicking in stunning mountains complete with waterfalls, with my parents, my paternal grandparents and my uncle and his family.

Then there were more school excursions to monasteries and historical villages, learning about famous revolutionaries and writers, and visits to museums and the theatre. I remember falling asleep in red velvet seats at the symphony orchestra in Sofia every month, forced to attend by my mother. But I also vividly remember hearing Tchaikovsky's Piano Concerto Number 1 for the first time in one of those red velvet seats at the ripe old age of eight and becoming quite literally obsessed with it; an obsession I still have to this day. I also remember the occasional Italian and French songs blasting out of neighbouring stereos and radios, particularly my favourite Al Bano and Romina Power and their song '*Libertà*'.

Time would pass, seasons would pass and the colourful carpets of leaves I so adored would be replaced by snow. I remember watching the first snow appear on top of Vitosha Mountain from my living room couch in Sofia. Soon it would be Christmas time again and that meant the return to Burgas for the two-week Christmas break. I remember going to the markets with my uncle and cousin to buy the Christmas tree, then dragging it home through the snow, or rather, the melted snow since Burgas, unlike Sofia, never really enjoyed much snow.

I have the warmest memories of decorating the tree for hours, and then the three days of celebrations, starting on the 30th December, climaxing on the 31st December, and concluding on the 1st of January. Three generations of family cooking all day, then four generations of family eating, drinking and dancing all night.

The big celebrations took place on New Year's Eve, at midnight, when we gathered around the Christmas tree to get our Christmas presents from *Diado Mraz* (Grandfather Frost), and *Snejanka* (the young and beautiful Snow Maiden, whose relationship with Father Frost was never explained to us or questioned by us kids). This would then be followed by dancing a traditional group dance—*horo*—with every single member of the family holding hands and jumping about the entire house, starting in the dining room, through the living room, along the cold marble corridor and back again.

I remember the New Year's comedy shows with Bulgaria's greatest actors and comedians, then the presidential address, and of course, the fireworks. But the celebrations didn't end there, there was the first day of the new year, when kids went around visiting neighbours to perform a blessing ritual, patting their back with a *syrvachka* made out of tree branches and decorated with all sorts of dried fruit and colourful ribbons, while reciting a blessing for health and prosperity in exchange for lollies, fruit and money.

Then more eating, some classical music concerts broadcast from Vienna, and running out onto the balcony to the giant barrel of sour cabbage to help myself to my favourite winter drink—sour cabbage juice. Do not comment until you have tried it, please. And of course, Bulgaria's magical sausages—*lykanka* or *diado*, and the world's greatest tomato, roasted capsicum and eggplant dip, *lutenitsa* on thick bread.

The 1st March, or *Baba* Marta Day (Granny Marta Day) in Bulgaria spells the end of winter and the beginning of spring. It's a day when young and old across the entire country exchange traditional good luck and good health charms, called *martenitsa*. We wear these woollen red and white intertwined figurines pinned on our coat or around the wrist as a band until the end of March, when we adorn the first blossoming tree we sight with all the *martenitsi* we have collected from loved ones. And before we know it, it will be the beginning of another glorious Bulgarian summer.

This is my Bulgaria, Bulgaria of the 1980s and early 1990s between Sofia (my parents' base and my school), weekends in Samokov (where my paternal grandparents had retired) and Burgas, on the Black Sea, where I spent all of my holidays, all four months of it, summer, spring holidays and Christmas break, with my great-grandmother, maternal grandparents, aunt, uncle and cousin.

Yes, I think it is evident I am bursting with pride and happiness every time I think of my family or my childhood. Okay, I exaggerate; there were some less than joyful moments. More precisely, those intervals during the year when I struggled to assert my independence in front of my extremely strict parents and when they punished this most proud and sweet of children. Yes, when I give myself such positive evaluations I like to do it by referring to myself in the third person, because I feel this way you might not notice it is me paying myself compliments, and therefore it will sound more objective.

Now I have let you into my world, my precious childhood, I find myself quite conflicted. Conflicted because while I loved writing all of the above snapshots, writing these ever so personal memories feels so self-indulgent, I find myself feeling a little embarrassed and I cringe. I cringe because, while everything I have stated above is true, I sound a little like the category of people we all know a few of, who are forever trying to convince us that their life is utterly perfect; and I cannot stand those people. I cannot stand those people because it is most un-Bulgarian to boast of perfection. Bulgarians do not much care for perfection, but beyond that Bulgarians across all layers of society love to complain.

This is our national mode of meditation/relaxation—get a small audience of friends or neighbours (even one will do) and complain to your heart's delight, but whatever you do, do not, under any circumstances, admit to being happy or satisfied. It is extremely bad luck and if you should accidently slip up a confession of feeling satisfied, you better be close to some wooden object you can knock on (other than your head) and cross your fingers and hope bad luck does not befall you. Bulgarians are always shocked to find themselves considered among the unhappiest Europeans, even though this is based on self-rated surveys. We are so superstitious about admitting to any level of joy, that even pen and paper surveys prompt us into complaining about life and ultimately sees us rated (self-rated, mind you) amongst the least satisfied of Europeans.

On a more serious note, Bulgaria in the years of my childhood and my teenage years did not stand for self-indulgent memoir writing, it stood for modesty, humility, education, respecting the elderly, reading books, learning, the arts, theatre, opera, science, poetry. That is what was valued, appreciated and celebrated. Unfortunately, this humility and modesty means that many of Bulgaria's great heroes and public figures have not left behind a memoir or an autobiography, and what a shame that is. It means that those of us least suited to this task have to take it upon themselves to try and explain the Bulgarian way and the great Bulgarian spirit to foreigners in precisely this type of self-indulgent memoir style of account. I am so uncomfortable with the idea of writing any kind of personal account in the form of a book, that I have even gone as far as to create an imaginary train and called it 'conversations on a train'. But, you see, I had to do this. I have spent two years looking for books on Bulgaria in English I could hand over to anyone and everyone who asked me about Bulgaria.

My aunt gave me a great coffee table book full of large glossy coloured photos of Bulgarian nature—mountains, the Black Sea, lakes, waterfalls, village houses; all stunning. But if you did not know anything about Bulgaria and you saw this book as your first and only reference, you would likely think that Bulgaria is a pretty country full of peasants whose only entertainment is a walk to the local monastery with their pet donkey.

Then I found a great book on Bulgarian civilisation on large glossy pages with a lot of photos. It covered all the glorious historical events and all sorts of inventions for which Bulgaria is famous (just not in Australia). It occurred to me, however, that the people asking me questions like: 'Do you have opera in Bulgaria?' and 'Can you own your own home?' generally do not want to be presented with a 500-page book written by an academic historian.

I needed a shorter, easier to digest account in order to get people excited about Bulgaria. I was ridiculously excited to find a couple of books in my favourite bookshop in Burgas—one covered what Bulgaria has given the world and the other book dealt with Bulgarian traditions and culture. Both were less than 100 pages and full of high-quality photos. Then I realised both books were intended for children and teenagers, and most importantly, were written in Bulgarian, not English.

Finally, at the bookshop at Heathrow Airport of all places, I saw a Bulgaria travel guide, which did not get basic demographic information wrong, judging by the first few pages. I got excited, thinking should I buy several copies. My frugal nature settled me down and I bought just one (and thank God I only bought one copy; they had forgotten to mention the Burgas opera house, most disappointing). But it still did not capture the Bulgarian lifestyle, the people, their eccentricities, what it means to be Bulgarian.

No one book could really capture all these facets and layers of a nation, a people. Yet I still could not shake off the overwhelming desire to tell my Australian friends and all Australians about My Bulgaria. And now you are here, so you will have to hear all about it too.

CHAPTER THREE

The big move to Australia

The romantic walk of my childhood you found yourself on a little earlier represents the essence of my childhood. This is how my idyllic, predictable, sheltered and stable life ran right up until the end of 1992, when my academic parents informed me that my father had been offered a one-year research position in Toronto, Canada and a three-year research position in Perth, Australia. This was not so unusual; my mathematician parents had studied and then worked (particularly my father) in foreign countries since they were 19 years old, dating back to the 1970s. This time was different, though, because both my mother and father had been discussing the importance of my learning another language fluently for some time (they were both fluent in four languages, with a fifth one a 'work in progress'). They thought it supremely beneficial to not only speak foreign languages but to be immersed in a foreign culture, as they had been during their studies outside of Bulgaria. Furthermore, they felt it was important I do that before the critical age of 18.

In 1992, my then 14-year-old self, soon to turn 15, took such job opportunities as a real threat to my happy, carefree Bulgarian life, and rightly so, because my parents informed me that we would be moving to Australia for three years. Australia was chosen because they felt that one year in Canada would not be enough for me to master English fluently and to really immerse me in a foreign culture, and that it would be too disruptive to my schooling. And so I promptly became religious, bought myself a cross and started praying daily that something would go wrong with my father's Australian contract and that there would be problems with visas or indeed anything else that would prevent this move.

I must therefore report that my daily prayers were not answered, and on 6th January 1993 the three of us, two highly adaptable, cosmopolitan, world-travelled academics and an angry, subdued, mildly depressed teenage girl departed the capital of Bulgaria, Sofia on a day when the city was experiencing record low temperatures of approximately -18°C. We arrived in Perth on the following day, 7th January, at around seven pm, where the temperature was approximately 37°C, down from 42°C during the day, we were told.

I made my entry on Australian land fully armed with some important swear words but in spite the three months at an English language school in Sofia, where we were required to learn between 50–100 new words a day, practice grammar and conversational English separately six periods a day every day, my English could best be described as below basic conversational English. There is a legitimate explanation for this—I was too busy not studying, as a form of protest and what I thought would be great punishment for my parents.

Putting aside the three-month stint at an English-language school, certainly my weekly private lessons in English at a language centre since the age of eight or nine could have helped produce some approximation of English language fluency, but as a child and then as a teenager, my main goal in life was to assert my independence in front of my parents. This, I worked out early on, was best achieved by doing the exact opposite of what my parents told me to do; more precisely, not doing my homework, not studying (except for history, my favourite subject), getting average marks, just to show them that they are not the boss of me, I am.

In spite of my supreme unhappiness with a three-year move to the other end of the world, I obviously felt I should still be documenting the ordeal from beginning to end and hence, began keeping a diary. My diary entry, in Bulgarian but translated here for you by the author herself, shows my first impressions of Perth, or rather the airport.

January 1993

'As we left the airport building the first thing I noticed was a big palm tree, taking regal place right outside. The building that houses the airport is not very tall and it is simply designed.'

I actually remember this very well. Not the palm tree or the actual design of the airport building, but the feeling this foreign scene induced in my teenage soul. It felt simultaneously exotic and isolated. The airport building was the single building in sight, there were few people, it was rather silent and there was simply bush everywhere. I come from a place where, much like the rest of Europe, the airport building is next to many other buildings, there are always many people in sight, it is never silent and before you leave the car park of any building, you have driven past many other buildings and many other people and you are approaching other buildings and people from all directions.

Two of my father's future colleagues from the university greeted us at the airport and drove us to our accommodation for the first week. My diary shows that the first thing I did, after I had a shower, was to put two photos on my nightstand—one of myself with my great-grandma and one of me with my grandparents and my cousin, who is really a brother to me, as we had grown up together and lived together for a good third of the year every year of our lives, at our grandparents' house. My parents were impressed that I had remembered to pack a few photos, because they did not. The experienced travellers they were, they only packed clothes, some books and academic dictionaries. All other possessions remained at home in Bulgaria, where coincidently, they still are.

It should be noted that my attachment to photos was not only a sign of sentimentality, and sentimental I am, but it is also a sign of my emotional dependence on my grandparents, my aunt, my cousin, not to mention my school friends, who at the age of 15, are so vital to a young girl's emotional well-being. Overall, a three-year stay in a foreign country produced a fatalistic outlook for this about-to-turn-15-year-old girl. In contrast, her parents did not think a three-year stay was long enough to require the packing of a photo album or a few photos. You may notice, when I recall memories that displease me, such as major life changes imposed on me (for example, the move to Australia), I am often tempted to refer to myself in the third person and so distance myself from the unpleasantness.

I should also point out that on our first night in Australia we were introduced to some local fauna—an Australian cockroach. Now, don't misunderstand, we have cockroaches in Bulgaria. It's just that in comparison with Australian cockroaches, the Bulgarian variety looks like a pretty light brown butterfly. The Australian cockroach, which we were later to find out can also fly, is between five and seven times the size of a Bulgarian cockroach at five cm long, it is practically black and long-limbed. I felt this was another sign that the move to Australia was a bad idea.

CHAPTER FOUR

First waves of culture shock and the Australian schooling system

My parents, especially my father, could not wait until the next day to explore our new surroundings and suggested a night walk around the university campus, which is located alongside the Swan River. Strangely enough, I remember myself being depressed to be so far away from home, yet my diary shows me to have been quite taken with the view.

'It was really dark, but as we reached the Swan River and the skyscrapers had all their lights on (apparently they stay on all night), and the lights are reflected in the river, it was super.' Super was one of the most frequently used words in both my English and my Bulgarian vocabulary in 1993. Even then I remember thinking it was wasteful but so beautiful to have all these hundreds of lights on. I had always associated skyscrapers with America and I always liked looking at them, but from a safe distance. I have never liked heights but skyscrapers in particular scare me; I find it so unnatural for human beings to be so high up. The top of the Eiffel Tower and the Empire State Building, both of which I expected would inspire my most romantic thoughts, instead made me feel nauseous, while tourists around me were yelling out superlatives about the awesomeness of the view. Having said that, I have no such issues with flying, probably because I started at the age of three. In fact, I really enjoy flying to this day, because I associate it with my trips back to my grandparents in Burgas.

This first night walk in Perth was surreal for my teenage self, because I could not understand how we could be standing by a river, staring at skyscrapers, all lit up, all of which suggests a vibrant, dynamic, big city, and yet there was not a single soul, apart from us, out and about. Not a single soul and dead silence. It felt like this big, modern city had all of a sudden been abandoned by its entire population, and somehow we did not get the message and remained, the only humans around.

Something else that made a lasting impression on me in the first week, again, according to my diary, were the glass sliding doors everywhere in every shop and every supermarket. In Bulgaria, but also in many old European cities, the shopping experience may at times be romantic (for tourists), but it is hardly convenient. You may encounter architecture from various styles and centuries all in the same street, and there are a lot of small specialised shops, but to reach them you usually have to negotiate a flight of stairs, either up or down; the doors are always narrow and heavy, and there are always, always, people either trying to go in or out at exactly the moment you are. This results in people either stepping on you or elbowing you.

Also, in Bulgaria (but I have seen this in Italy as well) the term 'wait in line' or 'queue' mean something different from what these terms mean in Australia. In Australia, a line means you have one person immediately behind another, immediately behind a third person, and so on. In Bulgaria, the term queue translates visually into the shape of a human triangle. More precisely, people do not stand behind each other, they usually stand on the side of the person in front, hovering over their neck, trying to 1) see exactly what is going on and 2) assess if the person in front is weak enough to allow them to push in. Since no one, not even people who favour the Australian model of a straight line, wish to lose their place in this so-called queue, they too move closer and closer to the person in front of them. But now there is more than one person in front, there is one on your left and one on your right, and so invariably someone will be perceived as having pushed in and invariably someone will complain loudly, but certainly no one will apologise or admit guilt. This is your regular Bulgarian shopping experience.

In Australia, and I have now lived here more than half of my life, I am yet to experience a scene like that. The doors open for you automatically, there are never, ever, any steps up or down, and there is so much space you are never tripping over people. Even more importantly, and surprising to a Bulgarian—people are always so relaxed that they patiently wait their turn. And I have never heard so many apologies in my life. Sorry is the most overused word in any shop or supermarket in Australia. If there is an item you are looking for, and the shop does not sell it or they have run out, the shop assistants begin by saying: 'I'm sorry, we don't have it.' It is so contagious that these days when someone steps on my toes or runs into me, I immediately tell them I am sorry before they even get a chance to apologise to me.

In Bulgaria, the term sorry, is rarely, if ever, used in a shopping context. If you get a nice sales assistant, they will say: 'No, we don't have it' and give you a little sympathetic smile. More than half the time, though, you will get the shop assistant who gives you a lingering look, head half down (because she is busy), eyes looking up, inspecting you, and after a careful pause, and with the most assertive and annoyed tone of voice (because you are bothering her), she will declaratively say: 'NO!' without a further explanation. Shopping in Australia is a little different, as you can imagine.

Then there was my introduction to the Australian schooling system. On my first day of school (after six months of studying English with other foreign students), within a few minutes of starting class, an Australian girl walked herself to the front of the class, touched the top of the teacher's head and loudly informed him that he was really balding (and this was a 'good' school in 'one of the best suburbs'). This is something else I learnt about Australia. Unlike Bulgaria, where no one cares where you live, in Australia there is a category of people who care which suburb you live in and that is often one of the first small talk questions you will be asked at a party. For many years I used to answer Bulgaria, just to amuse myself by confusing the person asking the question.

But back to the girl who outed the teacher as bald (because bald people never notice their baldness; they need someone else to point it out to them), I waited to see what kind of punishment such behaviour would carry in an Australian school. The teacher's reaction shocked me as much as the student's audacity. This old guy (to a 15 year old, an old teacher was probably someone in his forties) laughed out loud and made a joke, then gently asked her to sit down.

I was starting to relax about my schooling experience. Not because I had any desire or plans to feel the top of the head of any teacher, but because I quickly grasped that the attitude toward education and learning, and the student-teacher relationship, was significantly more relaxed and liberal than what I had known in Bulgaria. That is not to say that all Australian teachers would be happy to have their heads inspected by their students. But I had just arrived from a country where the student-teacher relationship could largely be explained in terms of respect and admiration at one end of the spectrum and sheer detestation at the other end, but never any hint of a friendship component. Friendliness maybe, but not friendship or equality by any stretch of the imagination.

To illustrate this better, imagine this: In Bulgaria, when class begins, you do not walk around the room unless asked to do so. The teacher would only ever ask you to do so if they are addressing you (by surname, by the way), wish for you to answer a question or solve a problem in front of the whole class on the blackboard. On any given day a Bulgarian teacher would teach a lesson for a part of the class, give homework, and examine either the entire class with a written test (test dates are not announced in advance) or they will examine one or a few students randomly selected at their discretion. When I say examine, I am referring to an oral exam, which is a foreign concept to high school students in Australia and even now, saying it in English sounds funny to me.

More precisely, a teacher would ask a question, either from the previous lesson or from any previous lesson during the semester (so you could be walked all over your entire semester's material without any notice) and he/she would randomly call out someone's name. If that name were yours, you would stand up and answer the question in front of the entire class. If the teacher was in a bad mood and you didn't know the answer, you would receive a two (the Bulgarian system follows the two–six system, two = F, six = A). This mark would be immediately recorded in your personal grading diary, which holds a record of all of your marks from both written and oral tests, for all subjects, and you carry this diary with you at all times.

If the teacher was in a good mood, he/she may decide to ask you another question, to give you a chance to get something right, and if you do, he/she may give you a D instead of an F. This poor mark carries the same weight as all other marks in that subject. During a given semester you will be examined many times and your grade for that term would be the average of all your marks. If you have received one F, your chances of getting an A at the end of term for this subject are slim; you will most likely get a B overall if all other marks you obtained in that subject were As. You may then beg the teacher to examine you, orally, on the entire semester's material in the hope that he/she may decide to give you an A overall, provided all your other marks in the subject were As.

Put simply, in Bulgaria, on any given day, every time you walk into your classroom, you face the prospect of being examined, either in front of the whole class or in a written test, on any part of the subject's material. Therefore, you can never be too confident or relaxed, unless you know everything you have learnt during the entire semester, for every one of your subjects. Furthermore, all subjects are compulsory—mathematics, Bulgarian literature, Bulgarian grammar, English, Russian, history, geography, music, physical education, chemistry, physics—the whole lot. At the end of high school, which I missed, you are also introduced to philosophy and psychology, as well as Marxism/Leninism (if you happened to be doing your final years of high school before 1989).

In Australia, by contrast, the usual grading format goes something like this, 40–60% of your grade in a given subject is derived from what is called an assignment. It's another word for a big homework piece, for which the student is given many weeks. The rest of the grade, 60–40%, comes from two written tests/exams— one a mid-term test (usually 10–20% of the final mark) and an end of semester, much bigger test, which accounts for 30–40% of the overall grade. Naturally, the student is informed well in advance when these tests will take place. Under the Australian system you may end up with a reasonable or even decently high overall grade, if you perform really well on the assignment component, while doing averagely on your two tests, which examine your actual knowledge of the subject. Many of my classmates spent most of their time working on their assignment and seeking a lot of help along the way from various sources and resources, such as parents, and older friends.

I was not complaining. Much to my excitement, end of year nine mathematics material (when I joined the Australian system with less-than-fluent English) had already been covered in Bulgaria in grade seven. I must confess I also enjoyed writing essays, even though the sentence structure preferred in Australia (but also perhaps in the English language in general) was different from what I was used to in Bulgarian essay writing. In Australia, English essays tend to consist exclusively of short and concise sentences; the simpler the better. Furthermore, it is widely preferred that the same term or word be used throughout the essay. In a Bulgarian essay you are encouraged to always use a different word for the same term, to avoid repetition, to ultimately beautify the text and to demonstrate a rich vocabulary.

In Australia, that will be marked as confusing and subject to misunderstanding. Furthermore, Bulgarian sentences are usually as long as a short English paragraph. I recently had to read something a friend of mine had written in English and I myself could not understand what she was saying until I cut each sentence into three shorter sentences.

Less study meant I had more time to be the angry, depressed teenager indulging in my new favourite activities—feeling sorry for myself, reading books and writing letters back home. It is difficult to imagine now but back in 1993, teenagers did not yet have email addresses or mobile phones. Furthermore, phone calls from Australia to Bulgaria cost three dollars per minute. Needless to say, my parents were not remotely interested in giving me an hour of talking to my grandparents and I usually managed a few minutes of supervised talk. It is difficult to complain to your grandparents about the parents who took you to the other end of the world when the parents in question are standing right next to you.

Letter-writing was something I enjoyed tremendously, because it was the one platform available to me at the time from which I could express fully what I felt and thought, and in those days, believe me, there were a lot of intense feelings and thoughts that needed sharing.

Every day I would sit down and give my family a detailed account of what I had done, what I had seen, what I had thought and what I had felt. At the end of each week I would post the weekly account, which often amounted to six to eight pages. I even managed to find really thin paper, which allowed a letter of 12 or so pages to nicely fit into a single envelope.

Yes, every detail, all the way down to the most trivial and banal was recorded and mailed away. This was highly therapeutic for me because I had a lot of difficulty explaining to myself how I could live so far away from my extended family for three full years. I felt that if my family could not actively and directly participate in my Australian experience, then I would make sure they knew every single detail of my life here.

Much to my excitement, I discovered that on the day of the arrival of my letters my grandmother would sit down the whole family for dinner—my great-grandma, my grandpa, my aunt and uncle and my cousin, and one of them would be in charge of reading out loud the entire letter.

CHAPTER FIVE

A 15-year-old Bulgarian's preconceived ideas about life in Australia

Truthfully, once we arrived in Australia, I was relieved. I was relieved because what I saw was not what I expected to see. Approximately six or so months before the big move to Perth, I had seen a long article on Australia in a magazine my father or my mother brought home from work; most likely the National Geographic. At that age I was not remotely interested in any article written in English, but this magazine had a lot of great photos, and photographic journalism was something I could appreciate even then.

From what I can remember, it must have been a piece on Australian farming because the images, which concerned me greatly (since I was going to that country a few months later) showed a lot of people riding horses, inspecting livestock, cowboy gear, a house in the middle of vast bushland and references to long-distance education (from what my limited English could decipher). I was horrified that I would arrive in Australia and would be taken to a house in the middle of nowhere, expected to ride a horse, surrounded by various animals and without much contact with other humans for days at a time.

I had studied about Australia in geography classes but again, that only helped reinforce the idea of vast spaces, deserts, farm houses kilometres apart from each other, rare and deadly animals and super-hot temperatures. Did I talk to my parents about what to expect upon arriving in Australia? Of course not. These were the people forcing me to go; I would not give them the satisfaction of asking them questions about the place.

My stereotypes about Australia, at the age of 15, were exclusively derived from one Australian movie and two Australian television series shown on Bulgarian television some years earlier. The Australian movie was *Crocodile Dundee*, which I saw at a Bulgarian cinema with my English language class, when I must have been 10, 11 or 12 years old. Thanks to this movie, I imagined Australia as a country of hostile vast bushland, crocodiles, snakes and men wearing rather large knives.

The TV series, which most influenced my imagination about life in Australia was *Return to Eden* with Rebecca Gilling and Peta Toppano. For some reason, I had always remembered it as *Return to Heaven* or maybe that's how it was translated in Bulgarian. Yet again, I learnt that generally people live in large houses located in vast bushland many kilometres away from friends. If they want to eat at a restaurant, they have to be helicoptered out of bushland and restaurants were generally located in the vicinity of skyscrapers. I also learnt, at 14, that if you happen to have a swimming pool, you would be wise to check it before you jump in, because your enemies usually drop small crocodiles in your pool late at night.

Finally, although I have always considered boat cruises the pinnacle of romance, I learnt that river cruises and boats are to be treated with caution in Australia, because a cheating spouse's favoured method of ending a relationship is to take you out on a boat and push you overboard into the always crocodile-infested waters. All I can say is, thank God for the TV series *Neighbours*. It was this show, shown on one of the Bulgarian TV channels in 1992, which showed me that in Australia it is possible to live in a suburb, with actual streets rather than bush, and to have neighbours nearby.

I was also mildly excited about the open plan living, where the kitchen and the living room are one and the same space. In Bulgaria in my day, (and prior to the year 2000) both houses and apartments treated the kitchen and the living room as two separate rooms. Cooking smells from the kitchen should never be allowed in the living room. If you happened to have a separate dining room as well as a living room, then again, they would be right next to each other but separated by a door.

It should also be mentioned that in a Bulgarian home, everyone wears slippers and that includes guests; shoes come off your feet the second you enter the corridor of someone's apartment or house. Another shock for me, upon arriving in Australia, was the sight of boys and girls of all ages walking barefoot in public. I don't mean walking barefoot on the beach—we all do that—I mean leaving their house to go to the shops barefoot. Admittedly, Europe is a lot dirtier and heavily populated, and Perth in particular is strikingly clean, but still, the sight of barefooted adults walking around the supermarket often left me shocked and amused. I had just arrived from a place where after a day at the beach, returning to my grandparents' apartment meant all of us, the children, my parents, aunt and uncle, had to take our sandals off outside, line up and walk across the cold marble floor to the bathroom, where one by one we would wash our feet from the residual sand, dry them thoroughly, and then and only then be allowed to proceed to the dining room for lunch. This rule applied to weekend living as well at my grandparents' weekend house a few kilometres away; a weekend house so low-key and rustic, as Australians would say, the furniture was approximately 50 years old. Even still, everything had to be kept clean to perfection and dirty feet would earn you such a passionately unpleasant lecture it was not worth the trouble.

CHAPTER SIX

The child and the state— Bulgarian style parenting and school

S peaking of unpleasant lectures, I remember recently hearing on radio a Perth female journalist talk about how shocked she was to find out that her five-year-old child had been told off by her teacher in front of other kids and how she would not stand for her child being publicly humiliated. Well, I can tell you that Bulgarian parents in general have no problem humiliating their children, telling them off in public, yelling at them in public and even smacking their bottoms in public. Bulgarian parents line up to buy presents for teachers who show serious strictness and discipline their child.

I was just about to say that this goes on right up until the child is a married adult and then remembered that even after marriage most Bulgarian parents I know have no problem telling their adult children off publicly and often loudly. In a Bulgarian context that is fine and accepted, but Bulgarian-style parenting in an Australian setting, I can assure you, is not so pleasant.

Consider this incident I endured. Although my English was limited in the first few months, my parents, particularly my mother, continued to enforce the same rules for social interaction and conversational manner that I had to comply with in Bulgaria. In Bulgaria, when neighbours or any other guests visit the house, no matter what the child may be doing, he/she is expected to stand up, join the adults and formally address and welcome the newly arrived adult, almost from speaking age. As the child gets older then a handshake is an absolute must, unless the child wishes to be branded uncivilised and badly brought up. The child is also expected to produce at least semi-intelligent adult-like responses to any questions directed at him/her.

The majority of Bulgarian parents (my aunt one of few who would never subject a child or teenager to such extremes) would not hesitate to publicly humiliate their child in front of guests by loudly correcting them and telling them off when they feel the child has underperformed in their social conduct. For example, a few months after our arrival, I was introduced to the Australian wife of a Bulgarian family friend in Perth. The lady extended her hand and said: 'How do you do?' to which, I nervously responded, 'I am fine, thank you and how are you?' My mother did not miss a beat and before another word could be spoken, she informed me rather firmly, right in front of the lady that the correct response to a 'how do you do' is a 'how do you do'.

Even worse, some years later at another social gathering, someone standing right next to my mother, who I had not yet met, had apparently made eye contact with me in anticipation of an introduction. However, I was busy looking for a chair to drop off my two heavy bags so I could free up my hands and shake people's hands. My mother, not realising that I was simply looking for a spot to drop off some bags, and horrified that I would not properly introduce myself and shake hands with people, raised her voice to a near yell and said, 'REGINA, get back here right this second and shake people's hands!'

The humiliation is only slightly lessened by the fact that she had done that in Bulgarian, however, I am certain her tone of voice translated quite well even for non-Bulgarian speakers, particularly if they had happened to notice her finger pointing. I rose up to the occasion by regressing right back to a rebellious, disobedient teenager and answered back, 'You can't tell me what to do!' also in Bulgarian and with as much attitude as I could muster. I have seen a number of Bulgarian parents chastise their children in a similar manner. I have never seen an Australian parent adopt this style of parenting.

My Australian schoolmates' parents were telling them to have fun, enjoy themselves, and to be themselves, whatever that means. My Bulgarian upbringing had taught me that parents generally try to mould their children into polite, responsible, modest, conscientious human beings, and 'having fun', not that that phrase was ever used, was something you did after you had shown yourself to be a good, responsible, studious child. If I was having too much fun, particularly at school, something was clearly wrong, the subject was obviously too easy and I clearly was not learning anything too worthwhile or at a high enough level.

In Australia this vital theme of having fun with whatever you do in life runs right throughout adult life as well. You will be hard pressed to find a public figure in Australia, or a prominent businessperson (businesspeople being revered in Australia the way scholars and intellectuals are revered in Europe) who does not identify fun and 'passion' for their work as a key factor in their success. Coming from a socialist country, working hard and achieving a certain level of competence was strongly emphasised, but having passion or, God forbid, fun with it, not. Work is to fulfil and stimulate you, to make a contribution to society and to generate income; passion and fun are constructs we associate with family, friends, travel and hobbies.

Robert Dessaix, who is my favourite Australian writer, shares an interesting and relevant to our chat musing in his memoir. Okay, I must confess here, up until the age of 35 I did not have a favourite Australian writer (much to my dear Australian friend Kirsty Hine's shock) but having read Robert Dessaix's memoir *As I Was Saying: A Collection of Musings* and five more of his books, I can now confidently identify him as my favourite Australian writer. It probably says something about me that my favourite Australian writer has a French surname, studied Russian literature in The Soviet Union in the 1960s and 1970s, then taught Russian literature at Australian National University for many years, and most exciting of all, has translated Dostoyevsky and Chekhov's works into English.

But back to Robert Dessaix's interesting musing. He talks about a Marxist writer, who I had never heard of (probably because I have not read many Marxist writers), called Paul Lafargue and his article 'The Right to Be Lazy'. In this article Lafargue argues that the 'passion for work' is a capitalist delusion, designed to enslave the proletariat by creating a 'sacred halo over work'. No wonder growing up in a socialist country no one told me I needed to have a passion for my future job; it's a 'capitalist delusion'. And how ironic to have a Marxist writer focus on our right to be lazy, I feel strangely excited.

May I just say how grateful I am I have discovered Robert Dessaix's most recent memoir, *As I was saying: A Collection of Musings*. I recommend it to anyone who reads books. He talks about the 'aptitude for idleness', and what a revelation that was to me, because I am convinced I have a great aptitude for idleness, but sadly, now that I think about it, I don't feel I have had many opportunities to exercise it. Perhaps I should work on finding a way to incorporate more idleness into my daily routine, and not just a bit of solitude, which I need greatly. And just how similar are these two constructs? Research should address the differences and similarities between the two constructs of idleness and solitude.

Over the years I have learnt that I crave solitude for a small part of the day, and I was greatly excited to discover that a number of prominent public figures also believe in the value of solitude. Mother Theresa said, 'God is a friend of silence. See how nature— trees, flowers, grass—grow in silence.' Then we have fashion designer Karl Lagerfeld, 'Solitude is the biggest luxury'. Acting icon, Sophia Loren, writes that true happiness is impossible without solitude. Diane Von Furstenberg also talks about her great need for daily solitude, and legendary Diana Vreeland takes the explanation further when she explains, 'When you are young you should be a lot with yourself and your suffering' in order for life to make sense when you become an adult.

Solitude I understand, but I had never heard anyone refer explicitly to idleness, let alone speak of an aptitude for it. This should be a new line of research for sociologists, because I believe that people from my parts of Europe—Southern Europe, Eastern Europe—have a natural aptitude for idleness, while the Anglo-Saxons I have met, not so much; they are always striving to be out doing things, joining clubs, rather than just being alone with their thoughts. They don't seem to have a natural understanding of the concept of idleness. In Australia I cannot go anywhere without being asked, 'What are you doing?' 'Do you have anything planned?' 'Are you doing anything later?'. In Bulgaria I am asked, 'How are you feeling?' 'What are you thinking?' 'What are you reading?'

Following this interesting diversion of thought, let us get back to Bulgarian-style parenting. I would like to say most, but I shall restrict myself to saying many, yes, many Bulgarian children and teenagers, right up until early adulthood, maintain a certain degree of mild or not-so-mild level of fear of their parents. You most definitely know your place as a Bulgarian child or teenager. In spite of my independent nature, my rebellious outbursts, not doing homework, skipping some classes and occasionally even arguing with teachers, all of which resulted in parental punishment, I carried a certain amount of fear.

Fear, like all things in life, is a relative term, so perhaps I should clarify. When I speak of Bulgarian style parenting and fear, allow me to say, it's not at all on the same level as say, the Chinese-American Amy Chua's style of parenting, as described in her controversial bestselling memoir on parenting, *Battle Hymn of the Tiger Mother*. I am reasonably confident I have developed an ulcer just in the course of reading about her particular brand of traditional Chinese parenting. Consider this—her children were not allowed to get any grade less than an A, not allowed to choose their own extracurricular activities, not allowed to watch TV or have a play date, must always be the number one student in all subjects except drama and gym, and the list went on. If the child refused to spend five hours—after a full day at school, mind you—of piano or violin practice, punishment would include being locked outside in the snow for disobedience and deprived of a meal. And if a hand-made birthday card was considered mediocre, she would throw it at her daughter, refuse to accept it, tell her what a poor job she had done, and demand she sit down and create a much better card immediately.

Therefore, when I mention Bulgarian-style strictness I have witnessed, it is only in comparison with Australian-style parenting I have witnessed, and not in comparison with, say Amy Chua's Chinese-style parenting, for example. Following this clarification, I feel I may freely indulge my further musings and complaints on Bulgarian parenting.

I was quite surprised to discover many Australian school friends considered their parents their best friend and often shared embarrassing details with them. Let me tell you, at 15 years of age, I was not confiding little secrets to my parents, I was hiding little secrets from my parents, particularly issues pertaining to school life.

There is one particular secret which has stayed with me to this day, although I did confess to my grandparents and my aunt some years ago, in my late twenties. It is so harmless and so silly, which is why it only further confirms what I stated earlier—the Bulgarian grandparent-grandchild relationship is all about excessive spoiling of every kind; the Bulgarian parent-child relationship, in contrast, has a clear military-like hierarchy and a dose of fear.

Now I can just imagine my parents hearing this or reading this account. My father would say, 'I cannot believe you wasted time writing this idiotic story,' and my mother would be highly displeased with her portrayal as a strict disciplinarian. I can hear her now, 'I won't forget this!' Read this with several exclamation marks, and she can get away with it, by the way. She can get away with anything because not only does she speak softly, and not only is she an academic in mathematics of all fields, but she looks like a younger Sophia Loren.

I should also point out that my mother will likely recommend I stick to the areas where I have obtained formal education, namely psychology, and not writing, or that I should take some writing classes over the course of many years before I attempt any kind of writing for public consumption. Fortunately for me, neither one of my parents is likely to be interested in my conversations on an imaginary train, and I may therefore proceed to indulge my most subjective of memories. Naturally, my little secret has to do with school, and again, it is not a short story (especially because it offers the opportunity to talk/boast some more about the Bulgarian educational system) but as always, I will keep it interesting.

Now consider this little story. By grade seven, I had changed schools and as a new student, without any friends yet, I was forced to sit right at the front of the class; a most unfortunate arrangement. In Bulgaria it is the teachers who move from class to class; your form class is the group of people with whom you study all of your subjects. Each form class is allocated a room and each student a desk and that's yours for the whole year, every day, for all of your subjects, which is why seating arrangements are important.

Sheer boredom due to an absence of friends and the undesirable seating arrangement, meant that I had no choice but to pay attention, and as a result, I actually started showing not only an interest in most of my subjects but I also found I was able to learn a lot during class, since I was actually paying attention. Almost overnight, the argumentative, naughty, notes-passing, skipping-class girl I had been at my previous school, became a straight-A student.

I had spent years trying to do badly at maths exclusively for the purpose of showing my parents they did not control me, and now I was top of my class and selected for after school special classes for more advanced students. My father, the mathematical prodigy he is, was never too concerned about school; he blossomed at university, but my mother was a high school gold medallist. Now, a gold medallist is not just a dux of your final year; a gold medal can only be obtained if you have been the single top student of your year for all of your high school years (my aunt, my mother's sister is also a gold medallist, so imagine also my grandmother's expectations).

If you do not acquire the necessary study habits and level of discipline at school, you have little chance at university. That was my mother's logic and she was greatly relieved when my attitude and my marks changed for the better. Especially because grade seven is particularly important in Bulgaria. It is at the end of grade seven that students sit exams to be admitted into specialised schools.

Students who are not academically interested or achieving apply for vocational specialised schools. Students who are more academically oriented can apply for specialised language schools or a mathematics specialised school. Alternatively, you may remain at a standard high school. The most popular language schools were the English, French and German language schools. Language schools work on the principle that students will study the same subjects as they would in a normal high school—history, physics, chemistry, biology, literature, grammar, mathematics (all compulsory) but they would study these in a foreign language (in English if at the English language school) from grade nine to grade 12. In order to prepare students for such an undertaking, they would spend grade eight studying nothing else but that language, six periods a day and the classes would focus on grammar, spoken and written English at an English language school, where on average, the student would be required to learn between 50–100 words a day, written, spoken and included in a sentence and/or conversation.

Please note, this is a Bulgarian educational initiative, these are Bulgarian schools and not a foreign import. I point this out because I have read a book on Bulgaria where the author mentions her French language school in Sofia and a British reviewer of her book had somehow concluded that the French language school in Sofia was a French import established and run by the French. Not so, although it was not uncommon to have actual French nationals teach at a French language school in Bulgaria, France being a rather socialist country. Approximately 20 percent of grade seven students qualify and attend these specialised schools and the entrance depended on your overall marks for the year in all your subjects (50 percent) and on your exam marks (50 percent) in literature and mathematics.

I was one of those applicants, even though by that time it was already known that I would be making a three-year move to Australia several months later. My mother in particular thought it would be a great idea, not so much because I was now a straight-A student but because she though the experience of sitting exams at a young age was important preparation for your future exam-sitting.

Here I was, all my teachers with their high expectations, the mathematics exam date is set, and the location for the exam is set at a school I was not familiar with. My mother takes me to this school. There are students from all over the city anxiously waiting and looking up their names to see which school room they are allocated to for their three-hour exam. Everyone is rushing (these are the nerds of the nerds, you understand) to find their spot. I find the room and by the time I enter I see that not only are all the front rows taken (amongst nerds at such an important exam front row seats go from most undesirable to most desirable) but the only available free seats are the last two rows of the classroom.

Ordinarily that would not be a problem, but one year earlier I had noticed that I could no longer read subtitles from my usual seat on the couch, and given that most members of my family are to some extent short-sighted, my father decided to take me to an eye specialist during the summer of 1991 just before grade seven started. It was discovered that indeed I was slightly short-sighted, one eye was −1 and the other just slightly under −1, but the eye specialist, a cousin of my mother's sympathised with my emotional reaction to this news and told me that I could postpone getting glasses if I sat close to the front of the classroom. I was delighted and as luck would have it, starting at a new school several months later, the front row was where I was asked to sit. However, when you have spent the entire year sitting right at the front and seeing clearly even though you are short-sighted, to sit at the back I realised I could only see a blackboard with a haze of white writing on it.

This is now 1992; we are still in the world of blackboards and white chalk. The exam is not a piece of paper in front of you on your desk; the exam is hand written questions in white chalk on a blackboard. Here I am, in a school I had never been to before, in a room full of students I had never met before, with an examiner I had never seen before, sitting at the back, realising that I am about to sit an exam I can't read. And most disturbing of all, I am not worried about the exam, I am worried about my mother's reaction and punishment when she finds out.

In an ideal world, the logical reaction would be for me to stand up, walk over to the examiner, however serious and intimidating she may look, explain that I am short-sighted but do not yet wear glasses, I cannot see the questions, could she let me swap seats with someone who does not mind moving. But that's not how the paralysed shy mind of a 13-year-old works and so my solution is to endure this nightmare by straining my eyes and ultimately making up the questions myself. Is this a five or an eight? Strain your eyes and then decide at random if you will treat it as a five or an eight. When you can't read the actual question, summon the psychic in you to predict what the question might be asking.

I am no psychic and it showed. I got the equivalent of a D. And herein lies my secret, I never told my parents, or anyone else for that matter, that I could not see or read the exam questions. This is a good example of the certain element of fear intertwined in the Bulgarian child-parent relationship.

If I had told my mother in particular that I could not see and I was too embarrassed to 1) approach the examiner and ask for help and 2) reveal publicly that I am short-sighted, she would be furious with me right there and then, for a long time after the exam and when I receive the actual exam results, and therefore it is best to say nothing and let your parents come up with their own explanations for your disappointing result much later when the exam results are announced. Fortunately, my high marks everywhere else helped save the situation and I was accepted into an English school, although it was my second choice of school and not my first choice of the oldest and 'best' one. I actually always wanted the second choice anyway because as luck would have it, this English school was located in the same building as my old school, where a big chunk of my friends were to continue their high school studies.

But think about this for a moment. Had this life experience taken place in an Australian context, that is with Australian parents, chances are, the Australian teenager would have confided in her parents and the Australian parents would have sympathised with her and promptly signed her up for some sort of drama class to improve her shyness issues or taken her to a child psychologist to address her anxiety about wearing glasses.

Alright, I must confess I have been waiting for the appropriate time to mention something about Bulgarian students, particularly students from the specialised mathematics schools, and hoping it would not sound like excessive bragging (we Bulgarians being rather modest) but it simply must be stated. Here it is—at the Tokyo International Mathematics Olympiad in 2003, Bulgaria finished in first place from a total of 82 participating countries. To be precise, Bulgaria beat China (second place finish), the USA (third place finish) and Russia (fourth place finish), countries that have respectively 184, 39 and 18 times its population.

Bulgaria also became one of only four countries in the history of the International Mathematics Olympiad to win that competition by having all six of its team members finish with gold medals. The other three countries to have done so are China, Russia and the US.

Inspired by these great Bulgarian achievements, I did a little further reading myself and found that it is not just 2003 that was a good year for Bulgarian mathematics students. You see, the International Mathematics Olympiad started in 1959 and since then approximately 100 countries send teams of six students annually to compete for the highest honour. Not only did Bulgaria win the Olympiad in 2003, but since its inception more than 50 years ago, Bulgaria has been in the top 10 countries 40 times, yes, 40 times.

As a comparison, the UK has been in the top 10 countries 24 times, France 11 times and Australia once. Bulgaria has been in the top five countries 16 times and, brace yourselves, between 1998 and 2003, Bulgaria was in the top five countries every single year. This data alone shows that whether Bulgaria is a socialist state or a capitalist state makes no difference, Bulgarian students will over achieve in mathematics, and I am certain none of these kids' parents were telling them to 'have fun' at school.

Let us not forget physics. In 2013, at the International Physics Olympiad (held in Denmark with 83 countries participating), the Bulgarian grade 11 student, Katerina Naidenova from a Bulgarian mathematics school, won the gold medal. I understand that it is not particularly important or relevant but I feel like mentioning that she is also absolutely gorgeous, wears red lipstick and fabulous high heels.

Speaking of female physicists I simply must mention that Bulgaria has 11 female physicists working at the European Organisation for Nuclear Research (CERN). While we are at it, indulge me as I share some more trivia, such as, according to Mensa International, Bulgaria ranks second in the world in Mensa IQ test scores and its students rate second in the world in **SAT** scores. Also, international Mensa IQ testing completed in 2004 identified the world's smartest woman (and one of the smartest people in the world) as Daniela Simidchieva of Bulgaria, who has an IQ of 200.

Now we shall casually slip back into our conversation about Bulgarian parent-child relations. The irony is that, as an adult, I see a strange reversal in this parent-child relationship. My Australian friends confide in their parents delicately and often through the use of diplomatic hints, and their parents, not wishing to invade their child's privacy, are reluctant to ask too many personal questions. Information between parents and children in Australia, compared with Bulgaria, is delivered on a voluntary basis. This, of course, is a generalisation but I mention it as a frequent occurrence I have observed with a number of friends and acquaintances.

Such issues generally do not exist in the adult phase of the Bulgarian parent-child relationship; old habits of demanding answers and constant invasive interfering in your child's life ensures that the child voluntarily or simply out of habit keeps the parent well informed on all personal and career moves.

When the Bulgarian child refuses to discuss a particular issue, unlike the Australian parent who would keep out of it and not mention the topic again, a Bulgarian parent will volunteer a long and extensive lecture consisting of blunt and brutal speculations as to why their child is uncooperative and secretive. Usually there will be heated exchanges and disagreements, raising of voices, rapid hand gesturing and probably several loud follow up conversations to clarify their position, but eventually the truth always comes out and there is a real and genuine sharing of innermost thoughts and feelings, even if these are sometimes communicated in a yelling and aggressive manner or, I should say, in a cleansing and cathartic manner.

As adults, most Bulgarians would confess to being extremely close to their parents and the invasive nature of the parent-child relationship, the constant talking and sharing, discussing, advising and questioning, certainly develop the habit (and eventually the desire) of sharing your thoughts and plans with your parents.

Something else that is typical of the Bulgarian parent-child relationship (and contradictory, like many a Bulgarian thing) is the fact that we love to complain about our parents and we disagree and argue passionately but in spite all of that, we still see each other or talk on the phone daily, spend holidays together and generally spend a tremendous amount of time with our immediate family as we get older. Many of us also do that with our grandparents, who in Bulgaria hold revered positions in a grandchild's life.

Grandparents in Bulgaria have the status of secondary guardians to their grandchildren and they are called upon to co-parent often. My grandparents have certainly co-parented with my parents and I cannot imagine having a closer relationship with them, had they been my actual parents. Grandchildren in Bulgaria do not simply visit their grandparents or do sleepovers, they live with their grandparents for a part of the year. School holiday time, which happens three times a year (two weeks for Christmas, two weeks for Easter/spring and three month summer holidays) is the time grandparents become parents, and the parents gain near complete freedom from their kids. The annual school holidays amounted to four months, which means that I spent one third of the year living with my grandparents, great-grandmother and my cousin.

My parents also stayed with my grandparents for Christmas break and Easter and three weeks in summer, but that means that for approximately two months of the year, during summer, they were child-free. So you see, when you ask a Bulgarian to describe or list their immediate family, they would include their parents, siblings, grandparents, first cousins, their parents' siblings (aunts or uncles) and great-grandparents if alive.

I was lucky enough to have three great-grandmothers until I was a teenager, and my most beloved great-grandmother lived to 97.5, which means I had her in my life until I was in my early twenties. I had to mention this fact, because it is precisely this little detail about my life that I consider to be one of the greatest fortunes of my life, to have grown up in a bubble of unconditional love with four generations of family around. In Australia, from what I have seen, this list would constitute the extended family. Extended family to a Bulgarian means including your second and third cousins. First cousins in Bulgaria have the status of siblings and certainly living together for a part of the year (at your grandparents' house) until early adulthood and throughout your grandparents' life, contributes greatly to this closeness.

Even today, as a married 37 year old mother, when in Burgas, I still sleep at my grandparents' place (with husband and children as well) instead of a five minute walk down the road, at my parents' place, where not only do I have most of my Bulgarian possessions, but also most of my clothes. I will spend a part of the day there enjoying myself or even reading one of my books, but for all important meals and bedtime, my family and I spend it at my grandparents' place or at my aunt's place nearby.

I even insist on sleepovers at the weekend villa (instead of just day-long visits), seven kilometres away from the main house in the city, where the furniture and general living arrangement is not so suited to babies or toddlers. I do this because when in Bulgaria, whether it is a month or so of the year, I insist on 1) observing the same routine I used to have when living in Bulgaria full-time and 2) my children growing up with the same routine in the same family homes. Both of these make me feel more grounded and generally like all is right with the world.

It is not simply the fact that, similar to Italy, for example, apartments and weekend houses are passed on from generation to generation and young people live with the knowledge that one day they will be responsible for and the owners of their parents' and grandparents' homes. It's the level of sharing your life and your living space with your parents and grandparents throughout childhood and adulthood that creates this level of family and home attachment.

Some say it takes a village to raise a child. In Bulgaria it takes an entire family of three generations, parents, grandparents, great-grandparents (if alive) and aunts and uncles. My personal parental unit includes my parents, my grandparents, my great-grandmother and my aunt. This is also why Bulgaria has as many female engineers as there are male, and why in general women reach the top of all professions considered male-oriented in Australia— because grandparents co-parent their grandchildren along with the parents. That and Bulgarian women are naturally brilliant.

This is not exclusively a Bulgarian tradition. Many Eastern and Sothern Europeans follow a similar model of grandparent-grandchild relations. Even the French send their children to both sets of grandparents for weeks at a time during the school holidays. I recently read the book, *Bringing up Bebe: One American Mother Discovers the Wisdom of French Parenting* by Pamela Druckerman who lives and raises her three children in Paris and I recommend it to all mothers and mothers-to-be as a study of cultural differences in parenting.

Pamela Druckerman, a former reporter for the Wall Street Journal, has written a most interesting book comparing American and French parenting styles and living lifestyles. Married to a British journalist and living in Paris, and a mother of three children, she shares her excitement and appreciation of the French system.

Pamela points out that, in her native America, while there are some good day-care centres, they are expensive, while childcare workers earn less than janitors, have an annual turnover rate of 35% and low levels of job satisfaction. In comparison, the French system is heavily subsidised by the government (parents pay a token amount, which depends on their income and varies from 50 cents to five euros per day). In fact, Druckerman points out that you cannot run for public office in France without promising either an expansion of existing childcare centres or the building of new ones.

Furthermore, and of great significance, is the fact that in France a childcare provider is not only an esteemed profession, it is viewed as a career and it requires specialised and extensive training in order to work in the field. A paediatrician and a psychologist visit the crèche regularly, but most impressive for Pamela is the food provided for the children. For example, she writes that lunch is a four course event, starting with a vegetable starter, a main meal with a side dish of cooked vegetables, a different cheese every day and a dessert of fresh fruit, all cooked by the house chef and the ingredients delivered fresh to the crèche several times a week. This description immediately brought me back to my childhood in Bulgaria.

In Bulgaria, during our socialist years (it is different now) we had a similar system to the French one described by Pamela. As a child, I had no such appreciation; what I remember is the several course meals I could never finish and a child carer always trying to force me to eat more. We always had soup, a main meal and a dessert. We had regular visits by doctors and dentists, although I do not remember weekly visits by psychologists.

Between 1994 and 1995 Dr Judith Evans, along with four other researchers from four Eastern European countries, Bulgaria, Poland, Hungary and Romania, conducted a study (with a separate analysis for each of the above noted countries) on the changing childcare system and consequently, the quality of childcare provided to children in the years following the shift from a generous socialist system to a market economy. This study is of interest to me because it provides data and references the state of childhood affairs during precisely my childhood in the 1980s before the changes.

Starting with maternity leave, a Bulgarian mother was granted (by law) 120 days of fully paid maternity leave for a firstborn child, 150 days for a second child and 180 days for a third child. After these four to six months of receiving her full salary and having her job position held for her, she is allowed to take paid leave, although at a minimum wage level rather than her actual salary, until the child turns one (up until 1985) and up until two years of age after 1985. Admittedly, most mothers returned to work well before the two-year mark.

Dr Evans also points out that there was paid leave for a mother taking care of a sick child and that applied until the child turned 16 years old, and other forms of benefits for parents with disabled children. I mention this in a chapter on parenting—the Bulgarian way because it shows that in the Bulgaria of my childhood children were considered a priority for parents themselves but also for the country and its future.

Consider this fact, noted in Dr Evan's study. Bulgarian nurseries (from birth to age three) are not only free, but the guidelines on their running are set by the Ministry of Health and the childcare providers are not just young women who love children but fully qualified healthcare providers. A class of no more than 25 is permitted and there were two nurses, two helpers and one educationalist (to provide some sort of educational guidance for that particular age group). The children had uniforms and a specific schedule each day.

Because the paid maternity leave was rather generous, most mothers preferred to stay at home and according to official statistics provided in Dr Evan's study, less than 10% of children under three years old attended such nurseries. In Paris, where Pamela's research shows many women prefer to return to work after three months of maternity leave, around 30% of babies and children under the age of three are in some sort of nursery arrangement.

Bulgarian kindergartens, also free of charge, were run by the Ministry of Education for children between the ages of three and six. Children received free healthcare, three meals a day and an educational program. Also, it was not compulsory to attend kindergartens and their maintenance cost was 1.7% of the state budget.

I also reference Dr Evan's study in order to illustrate that a Bulgarian woman was expected to raise children but also make an equal contribution to society by working full time outside the home. Just before the collapse of socialism, in Bulgaria the female participation in the workforce was 93% (in Hungary 78%, Poland 70%). We are not talking part time work or work from home or flexible hours. We are talking full time work. I was brought up with the notion that you don't only work to make a financial contribution to your family life and to receive intellectual stimulation, as important as that is, you also work to make a contribution to your country.

Bulgaria was an idealistic society back then, and that too is a little known fact outside of Bulgaria. This is foreign to many of my Australian friends, who talk about making a contribution to their family but never really talk about making a contribution to their country. They do, however, talk about something I find alien—the search for a job they are 'passionate' about.

When I think of the Bulgaria I grew up in I think of a place of noble values, where the core focus for ordinary people was on achieving a high level of competence, working hard, making a contribution to your country, respecting people from all walks of life for their contribution to society, and staying close to your family and friends. The 'passion' in life came from all other aspects of life, not from work. You were passionate about your family, your friends, about learning everything your country had to offer in terms of nature and cultural and scientific advances.

I think of a civilised society, where people's thoughts extended beyond their own interests. Yes, I was taught to think of a career that would suit my personality and that would be intellectually fulfilling but it never occurred to me that that job was something I needed to be so passionate about that it did not feel like work. To this day, when I meet people who talk about their work not feeling like work, I first think, hmm, pretentious, and then conclude they are simply insincere. If work does not feel like work, it is not work.

CHAPTER SEVEN

Bulgarian art, the royal connection and a visit to the mausoleum

Now that our conversation has covered a range of my own personal experiences and musings, let me continue your Bulgarian immersion by introducing you to something more concrete, in the form of fascinating facts about Bulgarian culture, starting with Bulgarian art.

Outside Bulgaria, perhaps the most recognised name for a contemporary Bulgarian artist would be that of Christo, or Christo Vladimirov Iavashev (sometimes spelled Javacheff). Christo is famous for environmental works of art all over the world and belongs to the Nouveau Realism movement. Since my understanding of environmental art is limited in the extreme, the best way to describe his works is to say that he creates wrappings for famous buildings around the world.

For example, he has wrapped the Reichstag in Berlin, The Gates in New York's Central Park and Paris' Pont-Neuf Bridge. He also created the 39-kilometre-long artwork called the Running Fence in California, and images of his works are in abundance on the internet. A documentary about Christo's work, *Christo's Valley Curtain* by David and Albert Maysles, was nominated for an Academy Award.

However, as a child of the 1980s, the works of Christo were unknown to me. Even now, I am more interested in his life than his art. For example, his art and life partner, his wife Jeanne-Claude, was born not only the same year he was born, 1935, but on the same date, 13th June. She looked extremely eccentric, with wild untamed red hair, while he looks sophisticated, refined and understated. They never accept money or sponsorship for their projects and he funds his projects by selling his preparatory studies and drawings and selling earlier works of art. Christo and Jeanne-Claude raised all of the 21 million dollars it cost to wrap the New York Gates of Central Park.

Growing up as a child of the 1980s, when I think of Bulgarian art the first name that comes to mind is Maistora (The Master), or Vladimir Dimitrov, who is considered the greatest Bulgarian artist of the 20th century. He was born in 1882 in what was the Kingdom of Bulgaria and passed away at the age of 78 in what was The People's Republic of Bulgaria in 1960. The main reason, I believe, he is so memorable even for children, is his use of bright colours. His artworks can lift your spirits and take you to a magical place of sunshine and innocence.

I am a huge fan of Chagall's work and I believe his use of colours is what gives his works real power. Maistora's paintings are more grounded in reality rather than fantasy, and his use of colour is even more intense and magical to me. I insist you immediately YouTube 'Vladimir Dimitrov—The Master' as this is the best clip I could find that captures some of his most famous pieces, 'Out of the Shell', 'Women's Prayers', 'Harvester Woman', 'The Wedding' and 'The Bulgarian Madonna' (which may be seen in a number of school textbooks).

It is also worth looking for images of these paintings online. If you look long enough you will start to feel as though you have been transported into his paintings. His style is unique and has been described as everything from fauvist to expressionist and post-impressionist, but as a Bulgarian I sense something distinctly Bulgarian in all his works; there is an element of Bulgarian folklore that is unique and this makes his works incomparable to other foreign famous artist of that century.

He is an interesting character, who reminds me of Tolstoy in appearance and also because even after he became prominent and successful, he consistently kept giving away his worldly possessions and insisted on living in near poverty, wearing only old rags and living as a vegetarian. Although he had travelled extensively through Russia, Italy, France, England, Turkey and America, he settled in a village in Bulgaria, and he is quoted as saying, 'if there is an earthly paradise, this is the area of Kyustendil, and its centre is the village of Shishkovtsi.' I have never been to Kustendil but one reason to go would be to visit the museum dedicated to Maistora, which houses 300 of his paintings and 1000 of his drawings (and more than 1000 other artworks from Bulgaria and abroad).

Now as a mother to sons, I have found another reason to love the great Maistora, his own love for his mother, who he painted throughout his life. I am happy to report that in 1982 UNESCO paid tribute to this extraordinary artist by celebrating the 100th anniversary of his birth.

Then there are individual works of art that remind me of my childhood because famous works of art were often used as covers for textbooks or classic novels. My single favourite such painting from childhood is 'The Old Plovdiv' (*Staria Plovdiv*) by Tsanko Lavrenov painted in 1940. It shows a nicely elevated view of the old part of the city of Plovdiv, with its multi-coloured beautiful revival-era mansions, with gentlemen dining in the front yards, ladies walking up the cobbled streets and horses riding uphill. I saw this favourite piece of mine at the Kazanlak Art Gallery recently, on a trip with my aunt, uncle and husband.

This highlights something else that should be mentioned about Bulgaria and the Bulgarian spirit that is worthy of admiration. Kazanlak is a small town of approximately 50,000 people. Yes, it is the centre of rose oil extraction (it is near the famous Rose Valley, which is where 85% of the world's rose oil is produced, including the oil used in most famous French beauty and perfume products), and there is some industry, but it is not Bulgaria's cultural centre. Yet this town has a magnificent art gallery, which holds more than 4500 works by Bulgaria's most famous artists.

Even more impressive, the artists themselves or their families have donated these works to the gallery. A book I bought about the Kazanlak Art Gallery informs me that the gallery opened in 1901, and in 1930, the famous Bulgarian writer and artist, Chudomir, became the gallery's director. From there on, some of Bulgaria's most prominent contemporary artists donated many of their works to the museum. The gallery even has a Vladimir Dimitrov painting, 'The Maiden'.

In my thirties I am still discovering Bulgarian artists to love and admire. Alexander Petrov and his 1967 painting 'Rose-picking' has me captivated, Vladimir Kavaldjiev has works that are reminiscent of Cezanne. To me personally, Anton Mitov is a true Bulgarian artist. Zlatko Boiadjiev, who has a Chagall-vibe (his early works of Russian villages) running through his works, and Nenko Balkanski are all favourites now.

My first independent experience with art took place on a sunny school day in Sofia in grade three or four, I believe, in 1987–1988. When I say independent, I mean an experience initiated not by my parents or by a teacher taking us on a school excursion, but by me and one of my then best friends. I have no idea why we decided to skip class (although I vaguely remember it was a biology class we skipped and it was the first time either of us had ever skipped a class) and catch the tram to the centre of the city, or why we decided to go to the National Art Gallery in particular, but that is exactly what we did.

Bulgaria's National Art Gallery is located in the centre of Sofia on Battenberg Square in what used to be the royal palace, and it houses more than 50,000 items. As a 10 year old, going on 11, I had no knowledge of the exact collection of art held at the gallery or the number of art pieces but it felt like a grown up thing to do, especially with a friend who happened to be the tallest girl at school at 173 cm (in grade four) and who was often mistaken for an adult, and even for my mother once.

This is one of the great things about Sofia, in terms of cultural activities. The National Art Gallery, the Gallery for Foreign Art, opera, ballet, the famous Aleksander Nevski Cathedral, and examples of architecture from ancient ruins to churches, communist monuments and buildings as varied as neo-baroque, neoclassical and rococo, are all located within walking distance in the centre of the city.

The National Art Gallery was moved to the former royal palace in 1946, shortly after the abolition of the monarchy, and this is where it remains. When I made that visit to the gallery as a young girl, I had no interest in the royal family, the House of Saxe-Coburg and Gotha. Growing up in socialist Bulgaria, the former royal family was not often mentioned for obvious reasons, and I don't recall having any fascination for these individuals or their fate. I do remember though that the interior of the palace felt cosy and warm, even homely, and I remember that the timber floor was squeaky and I thought how scary it would be to live in a place with squeaky floors.

I was not overcome by any grandness. Historically, Bulgarians have not shown a tendency for extreme extravagance. But as grown up as I felt in skipping class, the eye of a child becomes saturated by art in a shorter span of time than an adult and my friend and I left without seeing the entire collection. We must have left relatively quickly because we thought that it would be a shame to return to school so soon and wondered where else to go.

Standing outside the palace, it occurred to me and I explained to my friend that I had never visited the Georgi Dimitrov mausoleum, and as irony would have it, the body of this first of Bulgarian communist leaders was held in a mausoleum immediately opposite the royal palace. If you were to stand on the main palace balcony you could wave to the guards guarding the body of our first communist leader. The mausoleum was an understated white marble building and from the outside it did not look particularly imposing. I had always liked the somewhat theatrical uniforms of the guards and to this day I like to walk past the presidency building just to see their brightly coloured uniforms.

There was a rather long line of people of all ages evidently eager to catch a glimpse of Georgi Dimitrov and I remember feeling a little nervous at the thought of seeing a dead man. As we finally entered, we were guided to do a complete circle of a walk around the glass, presumably to see the body from all angles. But there were a lot of people on that particular day; it may have been a pre-organised group viewing of some sort, and I remember feeling that I hadn't really had a good look and I convinced my friend to go in a second time.

It is a surreal experience, particularly for a young girl, so much so, I still remember it vividly. I distinctly remember thinking that he looked very much alive and so well rested, like he was having a nice afternoon nap before getting back to important communist deeds. Then someone in the group around us, or maybe even a mausoleum official, made a comment about what has to happen to the preserved body daily in order to keep it looking so alive and well rested, and I remember feeling put off and suddenly needed to leave.

Either way, I am glad I managed to visit something that no longer exists. Not only are you unable to see the preserved body anymore, and presumably there would not be high demand for it today, but the building no longer exists as Bulgarian leaders of modern day have an uncivilized habit of demolishing things that they believe symbolise something they no longer believe in. I am told that, even though opinion polls showed that the majority of the population were against the demolition of this white marble building, the governing party of the time decided to go ahead in 1999. And this building, which could have housed a number of important science institutions, particularly given its underground facilities, was destroyed, and in its place we now have nothing but empty space.

But the building had the last laugh. It was built immediately following Georgi Dimitrov's unexpected death in 1949 and it took a record six days to build by workers who worked in shifts 24 hours a day. The demolition was going to be a great spectacle, televised and spectacular. All newly important democrats (read former communists) were in place, the explosives went off, and then nothing. The building did not even move.

If that was a rather embarrassing start to this symbolic gesture, it was about to get worse, because the second set of explosives followed, and again the building did not move. A third try resulted in a slight tilt but the building was still standing in defiance. It took four sets of explosives and bulldozers to damage it sufficiently to satisfy the democrats. And after this grand gesture of symbolism, as embarrassing as it was, this prime location is now empty space. Fortunately, this event took place when I was in Perth, Australia but in this day of internet glory, you may be able to see at least part of it on YouTube.

Now that I have shared these unexpected and spontaneous memories, I shall return to the original topic, Bulgarian art. This is how I, as a child and a young teenager, thought of Bulgarian art— Vladimir Dimitrov – Maistora (our most prominent 20th century artist), Zahari Zograf (our most famous 19th century painter), icons (especially the icon of the dragon-slaying Saint George) and of course, Thracian gold treasures, particularly the Panagyurishte Treasure.

Following the brutal submergence of Bulgaria into the Ottoman Empire in 1396, for 500 years the main form of art practiced in this country was iconography and woodcarving, mostly in monasteries, where monks kept art and our language alive in what you would call underground schools, and where scholars retold Bulgarian history and Bulgarian ancient literature.

In this historical context, foreigners can understand the Bulgarian fascination and love of monasteries and icons even if many do not consider themselves religious. Monasteries and icons carry significant historical value that reaches far and beyond religion. Bulgaria still has around 160 operating monasteries, which are regularly visited by Bulgarians throughout the year. In fact, the oldest operating monastery in Europe is the Bulgarian monastery Saint Atanasii the Great, built in 344 (there are a couple of French monasteries nearly as old, built in 373–375).

Bulgaria's liberation from the Ottoman Empire in 1878 was followed by an exhilarating period of national revival and striving to define and redefine all things Bulgarian, and Maistora's time was precisely then, after Bulgaria's liberation. He has acknowledged that he too, was influenced by Bulgarian icons and that his inspiration comes from the land of Bulgaria and folklore.

If you ever visit Bulgaria (and you should) and if you have the pleasure of staying at a Bulgarian home, chances are your hosts will take you for a long drive to visit one of our most famous monasteries, the Rila Monastery. This is a UNESCO heritage listed 10th century monastery established by Saint Ivan of Rila (or in English, Saint John of Rila), who is the patron saint of Bulgaria. Near the Black Sea you are likely to find many icons of Saint Nicholas (Sveti Nikola) because he is considered the protector of the sea.

Icons are the most common gift for children at their christening, and between my grandmother, my aunt, my mother and myself, we have a decent collection at our homes in Bulgaria and now in Australia. At the Rila Monastery you will see not only magnificent icons covering the interior and exterior of the ceilings, a vibrant explosion of mural-next-to-mural as far as the eyes can see (Bulgaria's greatest 19th century painter, Zahari Zograf is responsible for many of these works in the newer additions to the monastery complex) but also incredible wood carvings and iconostasis. YouTube 'Rilski Manastir' and you will see a three-minute clip of the monastery and Zahari Zograf's works. Woodcarvers from Samokov created the iconostasis, which is special to me because it is where my paternal grandparents lived after retirement and where my uncle still lives.

Apart from the unique murals and iconostasis, the biggest attraction is the Raphail Cross. Imagine a wooden cross just 81 centimetres high. It contains 104 intricately carved biblical scenes, not figures (there are 650 miniature figures), entire scenes, each enclosed in a silver plated frame the size of a thumb. This miracle of art and craftsmanship was achieved entirely with the use of needles. It took the monk Raphail 12 years to complete (1790–1802) and he subsequently lost his eyesight.

The Rila Monastery is particularly important also because it is the resting place of Saint Ivan's holy relics (more precisely, Saint Ivan's preserved left hand) and the last Tsar, Tsar Boris III's grave (more precisely, his heart is buried there).

In spite the fact that I visited the Rila Monastery twice as a child and twice as an adult, I never knew that, or if I was told, I never made it a point to remember. In recent years, my curiosity about Bulgaria's last royal family has been piqued, largely due to the fact that a school friend of mine from Sofia presented me with a photocopy of a book containing Tsar Ferdinand's letters of advice to his son, Tsar Boris III, on how to govern the country.

My recent studies show that Ferdinand was born in Vienna; a prince from a ducal family of Saxe-Coburg-Gotha, but grew up dividing his time between ancestral homes in Germany, Slovakia and the Austro-Hungarian Empire. His father was a first cousin to Queen Victoria and his uncle was Emperor Franz Joseph of Austria, and in general, the ducal family of Saxe-Coburg-Gotha had managed, through marriage or via direct election, to rule several European thrones in the 19th century, Bulgaria being one of them.

Following the abdication of Prince Alexander of Battenberg, the first crown prince of the third Bulgarian Kingdom, the Grand National Assembly went shopping for a suitable prince to become the monarch, in order to avoid becoming subsumed by Russia. Ferdinand was chosen and elected in 1887. He was the first head of state to fly in an aeroplane. It is widely believed he was bisexual and highly promiscuous, and unfortunately, he started the Second Balkan War.

Feeling short-changed by the Balkan League's division of Macedonia, Ferdinand ordered the attack on Greece and Serbia, which saw us being attacked by Romania and the Ottoman Empire. Bulgaria was attacked from all sides by its neighbours, all because of a quarrel between the Balkan League countries over the division of their joint conquest, Macedonia. Then World War I came around and Bulgaria sided with the wrong side. We were defeated and lost a lot of territory, which prompted the abdication of Tsar Ferdinand to a palace in his native Germany.

He was so unpopular a leader that the rulers of Hungary and Austria did not allow him to visit his own palaces in those countries, so he settled in his German palace. In 1938 he sent his successor, his son Boris III, words of advice on how to rule the Bulgars and it's straight out of Machiavelli's *The Prince*. 'Surround yourself only with the mediocre, always be united with politicians, bankers and big time thieves (but not small time thieves), they are always happy to have the opportunity to share what they have plundered with the tsars, when you are filling up your pockets with the country's money, don't aim to grab everything, leave some of the pie to your generals and to your ministers and remember that of all things in your kingdom the people are the least important.'

Bulgarians should not take this so personally. Ferdinand also wrote to his son to inform him that he hated his wife (the son's mother) and was out celebrating while she lay dying. This curiosity has lead me to the discovery, via my mother, of a great book, which has had wide success internationally and in Bulgaria for years. It's by Stefan Gruev and called *A Crown of Thorns* (there is an English translation readily available).

By all accounts, Bulgaria's last Tsar, Boris III may have inherited some of his father's traits but he was a different kind of monarch and he not only loved Bulgaria and its nature with a passion, but felt first and foremost Bulgarian, as did his sister, Princess Evdokia.

This is the kind of effect Bulgaria has on people. When the princess was living with her father at their German palace, she so missed Bulgaria that various court ladies tried to point out everything undesirable about Bulgaria, to which she one day said, 'Do not speak! You do not know what Bulgaria is. It is my country.'

As you are well aware by now my mind tends to jump through a number of branches of association and it is a challenge to follow a linear fashion of thought, which would be rather dull anyhow, but back to the main topic of discussion, Bulgarian art. My most vivid memory of Bulgarian art as a pre-teen in Bulgaria is a fourth century BC Thracian golden treasure, called the Panagyurishte Treasure (it was excavated by archaeologists in 1949 in the town of Panagyurishte, hence the name). I say Bulgarian art, because the state of Bulgaria was officially formed by proto-Bulgarians, several tribes of Slavs and Thracians, in 681 AD and therefore any Thracian achievements on what is modern day Bulgaria are part of our ancestry and history.

This golden treasure, which is believed to be part of a royal set belonging to Thracian King Seuthes III, is unimaginably beautiful and ornate. More than six kilograms of 24-carat gold, it contains an amphora, rhytons and a phiale, and you can see it right now through Google Images and YouTube.

This particular treasure has travelled the world but if you visit Sofia you may see it for yourself at the National History Museum, which is now housed in what used to be a communist party palace in the suburb of Boyana. It is close to my parents' apartment in Sofia and a place I have walked past many times as a child.

You would not only see historical artefacts from prehistoric and medieval Bulgaria, but also Thracian, Roman, Byzantine, Ottoman, national revival pieces, folk crafts, 20th century posters, icons and at the same time you will be doing a private tour of one of the homes of the communist leader, Todor Jivkov, who led the country for over three decades and outlived many of his Soviet counterparts. There is an old joke, which states that the Soviets were pissed off that the Bulgarians never invited them to a state funeral, whereas they have extended invitations to several Soviet leaders' funerals.

Beyond Bulgarian art, you may also enjoy foreign art in the capital city, Sofia. There is a beautiful neoclassical white building, which still manages to stand out, in spite the fact that it is located immediately behind the grand golden domed Aleksander Nevski Cathedral.

This building was the state printing house in the late 1880s, was badly damaged in 1944 due to Allied bombing, and was rebuilt and reopened in 1985 as the National Gallery for Foreign Art under the initiative of the minister for culture, Dr Ludmila Jivkova, daughter of communist leader Todor Jivkov. As a patriotic Bulgarian with intellectual inclinations and as the daughter of the communist leader, she managed to secure vast sums of money for the arts in general, including the mass printing of books and authors previously unpublished, the making of films, and for buying art. She used to have a salon at her apartment, where once a week, she debated and exchanged ideas with a number of Bulgarian intellectuals.

But back to the Foreign Art Gallery. In this fabulous building you can find an amazing collection of African tribal sculpture, Japanese prints, pastel drawings by Renoir, Picasso and Eugene Delacroix, and the biggest collection of Western European art (19–20th century) in the Balkans; 10,000 items.

Ludmila herself died a mysterious death at the age of 39, about which there is still speculation, that the Soviets may have had her poisoned, due to her pro-western and other un-socialist tendencies and interests. A recent biography I read about her suggests that it is also highly likely she died of a brain aneurysm, as she had suffered life-threatening head injuries some years earlier in a horrific car accident. Intimates of her father say that even he, at the end of his life, was not sure whether his daughter died a natural death.

CHAPTER EIGHT

Bulgarian music

Growing up in socialist Bulgaria in the 1980s life was filled with music. I am secretly delighted that this statement may be causing you a slight shock or at least a surprise. But it is the truth.

There was music on the beach, where young and old played cards or backgammon with their stereos blasting favourite tunes. There was music in the parks; middle-aged men on their accordions. There was music at the open theatres, music at outdoor festivals; loud, loud music from a neighbours' house first thing in the morning on weekends, music at home, music concerts on TV.

There were daily TV music shows featuring traditional folk music, complete with national costumes, set in picturesque villages. Then later on in the day, short classical music segments either from Bulgaria or broadcasts from abroad.

Late at night, especially during the summer months, there were all sorts of popular music concerts broadcast and variety shows. Throughout the year there were regular and varied performances at the eight opera houses around the country, at the many symphony orchestras and at the National Palace of Culture in Sofia, which houses a TV studio, a recording studio, nine multifunction halls, cafés, restaurants, bars, bakery, music shop, business centre, bookshop, post office, luxury goods shop, and a desk for booking and buying bus, train and plane tickets. You can tell I am a fan of the National Palace of Culture.

When I say music was everywhere, I am referring to an explosion of musical genres and styles by what seemed to be an endless number of musicians. There was classical music, opera music, folk music, *stari gradski pesni* (old town songs), Bulgarian pop music, Bulgarian rock music, even Bulgarian metal, and that's before we mention the foreign music, Soviet music of all genres, popular Italian music, French music; these were all greatly appreciated all over Bulgaria.

The foreigners I remember liking were Al Bano and Romina Power, with their songs '*Felicità*' and '*Libertà*', Belgium's Salvatore Adamo, Edith Piaf, and I still like the Russian military songs, for reasons incomprehensible to me (I choose not to over-analyse this one, in case I discover something I don't like about myself).

On his first visit to Bulgaria 13 years ago, my boyfriend, who is now my husband, was intrigued by our family dinners. Between the main meal and dessert and between highly animated, loud arguing about politics, my grandparents, my aunt and uncle and my cousin spontaneously stood up and started dancing when a particular song came on TV. He had just experienced my Bulgaria, the Bulgarian way, for the first time. This is what I want for everyone who is not familiar with Bulgaria. Bulgarians are open-hearted, warm, spontaneous, and we know how to live.

In the years of my childhood, Bulgaria had a variety of popular bands and solo musicians. When I tell Australian friends this, they wonder what the content of the songs was like and to what extent it was designed to sell the socialist way of life to its population. The shock that registers on their faces when they find out that heavy metal bands like AHAT were formed and recorded by the state-owned company, Balkanton, is priceless.

I wish I could show any non-believer the video clips from songs of the famous Brothers Argirovi, with their bright coloured t-shirts, and bold patterns, or Tonika and Toni Dimitrova's romantic songs about the Burgas beaches and our glorious summers, or the love songs by Vasil Naidenov and Lili Ivanova. I wish people could listen to Margarita Hranova, Bogdana Karadocheva, Emil Dimitrov, Pasha Hristova or see Rositsa Kirilova's Meg Ryan-like sweetheart quality when she sings about walking on the pavement barefoot.

Then there were the famous bands. Shtyrtsite are something of a Bulgarian Bon Jovi, Signal, FSB, Atlas, Impulse, Duet Riton, Karizma and Domino. I have provided a list of links to my favourite Bulgarian songs at the end of this book. The choices are from childhood mostly, which I believe will be a great introduction to your future passion for Bulgarian music.

In the name of objectivity I should point out that one of my school friends, let's stick to first names only, Vladdy, and my dearly beloved cousin have informed me that some of my musical choices reflect the taste of someone over 50 years of age. I believe the exact statement was, 'no normal person under the age of 50' would listen to that particular band. Having said that, my list of names and bands is comprehensive and an important introduction to the Bulgarian music of my childhood.

No one I encountered in Australia, either in 1993 when I arrived or later, had ever heard of my favourite Bulgarian bands, or popular bands in general. Imagine my shock to discover that Bulgaria is known around the world, and yes, even in Perth, for its folk music and dance.

When I say people in Australia knew of Bulgarian folk music, I am referring to middle-aged people, but nevertheless, people here knew; my next-door neighbours knew. I am happy to report that they are learning Bulgarian dances from a Dutch teacher. And learning to dance a Bulgarian *horo* (group dance) is no simple matter, because even Wikipedia will inform you of the Bulgarian folk dance music's 'complexity of its rhythms in comparison to Western music'. This is apparently due to the use of 'asymmetric meters'. I have no idea what that is, but consider this—Bulgarian music uses western meters such as 2/4, 3/4 and 4/4, but in addition, also includes 'meters with five, seven, nine, 11, 13 and 15 beats per measure (asymmetric meters)'.

For me personally, between the western meters I don't know anything about and the Bulgarian meters I don't know anything about, the Bulgarian ones sound significantly more complicated. All you need to do to convince yourself of this is to Google and watch some of these dances: *Rachenitsa*, *Pravo horo*, *Kopanitsa*, *Paidyshko horo*. I know only one such dance, the simplest one possible, *Pravo Horo*, and no matter what type of dance is played I adopt the three basic steps I know. Sure, it confuses and ruins the rhythm of the two people on either side of me but it is a lot of fun, at least for me.

I must tell you also that the internet reliably informed me that Frank Zappa has listed a Bulgarian album as one of his favourites, the 'Music of Bulgaria' (apparently the original 1955 recording by Filip Kutev).

As a child and then a teenager, I, much like the rest of the young population, was exposed to folk music from the various regions of the country. It is only natural when you grow up surrounded by four generations. There are also the unavoidable TV and radio shows dedicated to this genre. I even have friends who attended formal folk dance classes, but it was mostly something you would do to please your grandparents.

At that young age my otherwise romantic and sentimental ears had not yet developed a taste for this particular genre or to put it straight, I simply hated that kind of music, with the high-pitched voices. I did, however, like the women's traditional costumes, and these vary greatly from region to region. For example, traditional costumes from Western Bulgaria differ from costumes that represent Eastern Bulgaria or the Central Balkan region. Bulgaria is divided into 28 different regions, so there are 28 different styles of folk costumes. I enjoyed the dancing in such elaborate embroidered shirts or *sykman* (a linen dress), the skirts with the bright and embroidered *prestilka* (aprons that go over the skirts). You would never wear one of these in public or at home; they are mostly preserved at your home museum.

In a Bulgarian household, the home museum, as I call it, is a closet in the corridor of your house or apartment which houses everything your grandparents wish to pass on to you and your relations after they die. Many grandmothers will agonise over every woollen blanket, doily, embroidered bed sheet and everything else they may be storing for future generations. You know it's part of your inheritance if it smells of mothballs or other such and possibly dangerous substances designed to preserve such family items forever and ever.

My traditional costume is in exactly one such closet, and I have worn it once, around the age of eight or nine, exclusively for the purpose of a professional photography session, and dare I say, I was staged to look like a well-dressed peasant. My grandmother has the photo, I have the photo; everyone is happy.

Speaking of folk costumes, you may buy one yourself from the many tourist shops around the country, and this reminds me to point out that in addition to folk costumes and folk dances, other folk arts are still flourishing today, although obviously not to the same extent they would have been in the 18th and 19th centuries. For example, the tradition for folk pottery (it is still used today; it is not just for decoration), woodcarving and weaving and hand-woven rugs, or *kilim*, is still alive and well. I love the rugs from the village Kotel for their unbelievably rich colours. These will transform any house.

These days I have developed a taste for traditional folk singing, and I appreciate the exact high-pitched voices that used to make me cringe as a girl. I am filled with pride whenever I hear Valya Balkanska, the 71-year-old folk singer from the Rhodope Mountains. One of the 300 songs that comprise her repertoire, '*Izlel e Delyu Haidytin*', is part of the Voyager Golden Record, which means that her voice will be heard in space for many more thousands of years.

I knew that the Bulgarian State Radio and Television Female Vocal Choir, founded by the famous Bulgarian composer Filip

Kutev (1903–1982) had received recognition across Europe but I had no idea that their 1975, 13 song album, '*Le Mystere des Voix Bulgare*' (The Mystery of Bulgarian Voices), had topped the charts and won a Grammy. Imagine the ultimate trophy of musical success in the most capitalist of all capitalist countries, United States of America, awarded not only to a choir from a socialist country, but to the official female choir of that socialist country. The album was introduced to the West by the Swiss ethnomusicologist Marcel Cellier who is also a producer, and his label released the album in 1975. Then in 1986 it was released in the UK by the 4AD label, and the following year 1987 in the US by the Nonesuch label.

I also did not know that Bulgarian folk ensembles invariably win gold or first place at just about every international folk festival or competition. Recently, I read that folk dance ensemble Sofia-6 has won three world folk competitions in the space of 1.5 years, in Cheonan, South Korea, in Bursa, Turkey (having won at the same competition in 2010 against 21 countries) and the 13th International Folk competition in Palma de Majorca, Spain.

I should also point out that we use a wide variety of unique instruments, the names of which I know but often cannot tell the difference between them, even though they not only look different but produce different sounds as well. For example, we have *gaida* (goatskin bagpipe), *gadulka* (string instrument), *tupan* (like a drum worn over the shoulder and for which one side is hit with a thin stick, the other side with a beater), *tarabuka* (finger drum in the shape of an hourglass), *kaval* (end-blown flute), and *tambura* (metal strung lute with a long neck).

I sense that the names of these instruments alone are arousing an interest and a simple Google search will generate not only photos, but video clips with musicians playing these instruments, which will no doubt be better than my limited descriptions. I should add the guitar, saxophone, clarinet, accordion, drums and the violin are also commonly played in the country.

Given my complete disinterest in folk music as a young girl, I have never attended the famous Koprivshtitsa National Music Festival. In 1965 the Socialist Ministry of Culture founded this National Music Festival in this most romantic, most beautiful village, Koprivshtitsa, and it still takes place every five years. I last visited this magical place on a primary school excursion in the late 1980s. As a side note, when you visit Koprivshtitsa you can also visit the 1830s house of the famous poet, Dimcho Debelianov. It is a museum now.

Bulgaria is a country with a rich and diverse contribution to world music and I wish that was more widely known in Australia. This feels like an appropriate place to engage in some more Bulgarian praising and I will begin by pointing out that Bulgaria has given the opera world three of its greatest opera singers—Boris Christoff, who has been termed the greatest bass opera singer of the 20th century, operatic soprano Gena Dimitrova and lirico-spinto soprano Raina Kabaivanska. Boris Christoff (1914–1993) was considered one of the best, if not the best bass opera singers of the 20th century and he was famous for roles such as Mussorgsky's Tsar *Boris Godunov*, Verdi's Phillip II in *Don Carlo* and Ivan Susanin in Glinka's *A Life for The Tsar*.

What is most exciting for me is that Boris Christoff, in addition to being one of the greatest in the opera world, was also a singer of choral music. My personal favourite is *The Russian Orthodox Christmas Carol* by Bortnyansky, which Christoff sang with the choir of the Alexander Nevsky Cathedral in Sofia, Bulgaria. A few weeks ago, purely by chance, I found Boris Christoff's biography, written by a prominent Bulgarian academic and translated in English at Elizabeth's second-hand bookshop in Perth.

Raina Kabaivanska, who is now 79 years old and still working as a Professor of Music in Italy, is considered one of the most talented sopranos of her generation. Kabaivanska is most famous for her roles in Verdi and Puccini operas. She sang nine of Verdi's operas and three of Puccini's. As an interesting piece of trivia, Raina Kabaivanska opened the funeral mass for Pavarotti in 2007 with a performance of 'Ave Maria' from Verdi's *Otello*. Pavarotti himself said of her: 'the past is Tosca of Maria Callas, Tosca of our time is Raina Kabaivanska'.

Gena Dimitrova is another legendary Bulgarian opera singer (1941–2005), most recognised for her role of Turandot in Puccini's opera of the same name. The great Herbert von Karajan stated, 'I have lived to hear a voice that only gods deserve.' An interesting fact is that in 1983/1984 Dimitrova was declared the best singer at La Scala and she was awarded the Giacomo Puccini Prize for her interpretation of the main characters from Puccini's operas, an award previously only given to Italian opera singers.

CHAPTER NINE

Bulgarian Film and TV

My dearly beloved cousin, Georgi, has often stated that he thinks I live in the past. Well, allow me to quote Faulkner, 'The past is never dead. It's not even past.'

What Georgi really means is that I often reminisce about our childhood, which was magical to me and I tend to be highly sentimental. I may get lost in my own suburb, confusing street names, but I will remember conversations I have had with friends and sometimes strangers 10, 15 and even 20 years ago, if the conversation was about their families, their feelings and their opinions.

These are the things I remember—songs, books, art, films. For me, they are always linked to particular episodes from my personal life, which makes them all the more important and special to me.

It occurred to me that a good way of showing off the Bulgarian spirit, as well as Bulgarian cinematic and directorial talent, would be to show people Bulgarian films. More precisely, old classics, old classics that were not filmed with a foreign audience in mind and trying to sell a particular politically correct and fashionable point of view, but real Bulgarian films focused on purely the human story, where, if politics were mentioned, it was incidental to the story.

What better way to catch a glimpse of Bulgarian nature, Bulgarian architecture, fashion, food, housing and lifestyle all at the same time, even in the absence of subtitles. Although I can imagine most foreigners would still prefer to watch a movie they can understand.

When I was a child, the Bulgarian film industry was thriving and the main studio, the Boyana Studio, was and continues to be one of the largest in Europe. These days a lot of Hollywood films, rather than Bulgarian movies, are being filmed and the setting often passes for a wide variety of European and even American locations.

In fact, if you Google 'list of Bulgarian films' you will be able to see year by year how many Bulgarian movies were released, as well as the titles of the movies. For example, in the 1950s it was a few movies a year, in the 1960s, on average close to 10 movies annually.

In the early 1970s on average 15 movies, but by the late 1970s, 26 Bulgarian movies were released annually. That is a new Bulgarian movie every two weeks of the year.

In the 1980s it slowed down to a few movies a year, and following the changes in the 1990s, no Bulgarian movies were made. Now in the 2010s it is back to a few movies a year.

I have a lot of favourites but I would like to list the real classics, films that have stood the test of time, not only in Bulgaria but with a European audience as well.

Although we have a number of great comedies and light-hearted movies, the movies considered Bulgarian classics would classify as beyond heavy viewing. Herein lies my problem; I am trying to excite the reader about Bulgarian films but if I begin with the real classics I will depress and/or possibly traumatise you.

The Goat Horn, for example is a 1972 movie set in the 18th century and it is about a father who raises his daughter as a boy with the singular purpose of revenge, or rather avenging his wife's brutal rape and murder, which he and his daughter witnessed. *Time of Violence* is set in the 17th century and is about the kidnapping of Bulgarian boys by Ottoman Turks and raising them as Muslims. But before you get discouraged, these are movies to watch in order to experience this art form at its best in terms of directing, story and acting.

Other famous classics are a little heavy, but not quite tragic. *Tobacco* (*Tiutiun*), *Doomed Souls* (*Osadeni Dyshi*), and *The Peach Thief* are also considered to be among the greatest Bulgarian films of all time and there is great love and great loss, happiness and sadness, splashes of tragedy and comedy all rolled into one, and never a Hollywood-style sweet ending. These movies are incredibly moving to a thinking person and the acting skills, as well as the directorial skills, show you that this is indeed art and not entertainment.

I would also like to recommend the 1979 movie *The Unknown Soldier's Patent Leather Shoes*, an intensely personal film by one of Bulgaria's most internationally awarded directors, Rangel Valchanov. Valchanov's work has consistently been recognised as non-conformist, and often a source of annoyance to the communist regime, but thankfully the state did fund his most personal film, *The Unknown Soldier's Patent Leather Shoes*.

Bulgaria can also offer great light-hearted movies too. My personal favourites are *A Nameless Band, Ladies' Choice*, and for children, I love *With Children at the Sea*, which I show my children on DVD often (but they are not as interested yet as I had hoped).

The movies I personally like and have enjoyed watching are *Tarnovskata Tsaritsa, Under the Yoke* (adaptation of Ivan Vazov's classic novel), *Illusion*. If I were you, I would aim to watch all of the movies listed at the end of the book in my resources chapter, (included here to simplify your immersion in Bulgarian culture).

Bulgaria's most beloved actors (and that applies not only to my grandparents' generation, my parents' generation and my generation, but all past and future generations as well) are the famous foursome, Stoyanka Mutafova, Tatiana Lolova, Georgi Kaloyanchev and Georgi Partsalev; all character actors of profound talent. I had the great fortune to see Stoyanka Mutafova perform at a theatre in Burgas some years ago when she was 84 years old. Her extraordinary gift, recognised internationally, is so moving it will reduce you to tears.

Coincidentally, seeing her after the performance, I was struck by how different she looked, how drained, and it occurred to me that while she is on stage she is possessed by the acting gods, and when she leaves the stage she is left to recover from the immensity of her own performance. In addition to theatre, she has appeared in countless movies over many decades but perhaps the most famous would be *Toplo* (*Hot*, 1978), *Kit* (*Whale*, 1970), *Tochka Parva* (1956). In 2015, at 93 years old, she was still performing on stage.

I would also like to introduce you to one of our most distinguished and talented actors of the generation following the fabulous foursome, Stefan Danailov. A theatre, film and TV actor, he is most famous for his roles in the films *The Black Angels* (*Chernite Angeli*, 1970), *Ladies' Choice* (*Dami Kaniat*, 1980), *The Queen of Turnovo* (*Tarnovskata Tsaritsa*, 1981) and the hit TV series *At Each Kilometer* (*Na Vseki Kilometar*, 1969). Even today in his 70s he has retained his incredible charisma. A few of these films, as indicated above, can be viewed in their entirety on YouTube, but sadly, they do not have subtitles.

In terms of directors, the most prominent are Ludmil Staikov, Rangel Vulchanov, Binka Zhelyazkova, Hristo Ganev, Hristo Piskov and from the younger generation I have read a lot of praise for Zornitsa Sophia.

The website vbox5.com provides short clips and in Bulgaria **www.zamunda.net** comes highly recommended. Sadly however, most films do not come with English subtitles, although newer films do. The Bulgarian National Archive can be found on **http://bnf.bg/.**

But enough about movies, let us talk TV for a moment. I have met people in Australia who genuinely think, although they would admit they have not given the topic that much thought, that TV in a communist country, any communist country, would be predominantly live streaming of Soviet news, Marxist-Leninist speeches and communist parades. They don't imagine a TV industry of any kind.

Of course, if one wishes to know exactly what was watched on TV, one could go to the library and dig up an old newspaper, learn some Bulgarian or easier, find a Bulgarian and read the TV guide section. Most foreigners would not have any incentive to go to such effort.

In this day and age, of course, you don't need to make the trip to the library, you just need the right internet resources or in your case, you just need me. I have chosen a random and fun date – January 1–2, 1979 (when I was a baby, well before the 70 cable Bulgarian and foreign channels we get now in most Bulgarian households). Let's have a look at the two main channels—Channel 1 and Channel 2.

Channel 1

MONDAY 1 JANUARY

10.00	Folk music
10.15	*My Childhood* (a children's programme)
13.15	Vienna Symphony Concert, direct from Vienna
14.30	Continuation of New Year's Eve Concert
15.55	Children's animated film
16.05	Popular Music Concert from Central Soviet TV
17.30	News
17.40	Lotto
17.45	Cuban Ambassador to Bulgaria speech
17.55	*I Am Cuba* (documentary)
18.20	*Cowboy in the City* (animated film)
18.30	Musical spectacle '*Leshnikat Krakatyr*'
19.50	Good Night for Children
20.00	News from Around the World and at Home
20.30	Night Melodies
21.00	Continuation of New Year's Eve parade
22.00	*Stari Gradski Pesni* (Old Town Songs)
23.00	Spanish Movie
23.45	News

Channel 2

16.20	Folk Music and Humour
17.00	Soviet musical
17.30	International Tournament for Ski-Jump
19.30	Bulgarian Television Competition for Best Anecdote

19.45   *Diksyland-78* (programme from Dresden, Germany)
20.25   World Championship for Latin American Dancing
21.20   *The Importance of Being Earnest* (adaptation of Oscar Wilde's play)
23.00   Jazz concert

The following two days feature a documentary about the Atlantic Ocean, a documentary about unions, a documentary about a Bulgarian art gallery on its 30th anniversary, a documentary about Bulgarian suburbs, an Andreas Holm recital, a Bulgarian TV series, a Polish film, a Romanian film and again a lot of short musical programmes. The overall impression is that the two main channels in the 1970s covered world and local news, a lot of documentaries, some sport, foreign and Bulgarian films and series and a variety of different musical genre concerts, as well as theatre performances shown on TV.

It should also be remembered that back in those days TV was not watched the way it is watched today. If you weren't working or studying, you were spending time with family and friends and playing outdoors. Your TV viewing was for quality programmes, not for hours of background noise and mindless watching.

What is interesting to me is what Bulgarians who were old enough to watch TV in the 1970s think about TV options back then and TV options in today's world of more than 70 cable channels. Young people in their twenties seem to think that it's 'tragic' to only have two main TV channels, while people in their early forties and older miss a lot of the TV choices from those years. 'There was something for everyone; excellent movies, excellent series, a lot of classical music, a lot of documentaries, and now it's 100 channels of pop folk, action and commercials.' Yes, I like to read people's comments. It is a great source of information about society today and it can be both highly amusing and disturbing.

CHAPTER TEN

Bulgarian humour, anecdotes, fairy tales and adult literature

For as long as I can remember, and certainly even before I could read, I have been obsessed with books, their covers, their smell, and most importantly, the yet-to-be-discovered secrets they would reveal. And for as long as I can remember, even before I could write, I was asking for journals and diaries and desired to record all my thoughts and feelings on anything and everything I saw, heard and imagined.

When I was a little girl, I used to visit my paternal grandparents on weekends in a town one hour outside Sofia, Samokov, where they had retired. One particular year, maybe it was 1987 or 1988, just before making my way to Burgas to spend the three-month summer holiday with my maternal grandparents, I was visiting Samokov again, this time for a week.

I was beyond excited to discover that there was a library immediately outside their front door, less than 200 metres away; a library I had never noticed before. Even more exciting, my aunt happened to work there. Given my obsession with books, a profession like a librarian sounded exciting to me, particularly when you consider that almost my entire family was comprised of academics in spheres rather dull to my pre-teenage self.

My parents, as you now know, are mathematics academics, my mother's sister is an academic and engineer who married another engineer, my father's brother is an engineer and so is my paternal grandfather, my maternal grandmother is an accountant and my grandfather an economist. One of my three first cousins is also an engineer, his brother a PhD in computer science and software engineering and my youngest cousin holds two masters degrees and a PhD in molecular biology.

To me, an exotic profession was that of my paternal grandmother—a theatre actress (who coincidently I look like) and my uncle's wife—a librarian. So every single morning around nine am, I would make the short trip to this cosy magical place with a giant white statue at the entrance and I would roam this room full of books from floor to ceiling, and I would force the handful of librarians into conversation with me. I referred to myself as their colleague and I would hang around reading books, surrounded by books floor to ceiling and squeaky wooden floors.

Eventually, the librarians decided to utilise me and asked me to place library stamps on the large pile of new books. I could not have felt any more important and to this day, think of this one week as my first job. In the early afternoon, when I finished my 'shift', I would make the walk back to my grandparents' place and after my granddad had finished his chess games at his local club, we would all walk to my great-grandmother's little cottage house (my father's grandmother) where I would pick pears from her pear tree, admire her roses, and go through all her boxes of old letters and postcards from days long gone and ask questions.

By sunset my grandparents and I would be back at their place and we would do what I loved best—read Bulgarian jokes from the capital of Bulgarian humour, *Gabrovo*. This little yellow hard covered book was read and reread at every one of my visits and when they passed away I took it upon myself to consider this little book mine.

I include here some of these Bulgarian jokes, humbly translated from Bulgarian by me. Gabrovo is a picturesque town located where the river Yantra flows, and although it is a highly industrialised town, it also sports 14,000 statues. It was the capital city of humour during the socialist era, and as such, it hosted many international comedy festivals during which both Eastern European and Western Europeans participated. This is something else you would not think you would find in a socialist country, international comedy festivals, but we had them. As you read on, you will notice the jokes from this region tend to be about frugality and general cheapness.

'A waiter tells his boss that a client has complained that he had found a snail in his food. The boss tells the waiter, 'Lucky you told me, now charge him for the snail too.'

'A wealthy man from Gabrovo was travelling on a train in third class. It was a very hot summer's day and the train was crowded. A baffled gypsy travelling in third class asked the Gabrovo gentleman, "Sir, why are you travelling in third class?" The Gabrovo man answered, "Because there isn't a fourth class."'

'A Gabrovo man was hoping for free medical advice from a doctor friend of his he had just happened to bump into on the street. "Doc, what do you do when you catch a cold?" The doctor, also from Gabrovo, said, "I sneeze."'

'A man took his wife to the doctor's to have her tonsils removed. The doctor informed him that his wife's tonsils should have been removed when she was a child. The husband replied, "In that case, send the bill to my in-laws, please."'

While the famous Gabrovo jokes are about cheapness and frugality, jokes from another famous region in and around Sofia, called *Shopski* jokes, tend to make fun of Bulgarians from that region who are generally thought to be stubborn ('wooden heads'), dogmatic and sly.

'A tourist approached two police officers on duty in Sofia and asked them a question in English. The policemen did not understand him, so he asked them the same question in French. Again, the policemen did not understand him. Finally, the tourist asked them the question in German. Yet again, neither of the Bulgarian policemen understood him and he walked off, frustrated. One of the policemen turned to his colleague and said, "You know, maybe we should learn another language, it might be helpful." The second policeman answered, "Why? That tourist knew several languages and that didn't help him in the slightest."

Bulgarian jokes often go hand in hand with Bulgarian proverbs. People sitting in cafés, sharing their sorrows and joys, will often throw in a joke or a proverb. Certainly there are Bulgarian proverbs that have an English equivalent, but more interesting to me are the sayings that summarise what is most typical of the Bulgarian psyche and our way of viewing life and the world.

Bulgarians, especially compared with Australians, have a fatalistic streak and we have a saying you won't be hearing in Australia, 'If things are going really good, that cannot be good.' If everything is great we feel that some disaster is approaching.

In Australia when you wish someone a good weekend, they almost always respond with, 'Oh, I will, thank you!' Now, how do they know they will have a good weekend, and how presumptuous! They were tempting fate, I used to think. You wish any Bulgarian a nice weekend and you will always get one of the following responses: 'Oh, I really hope so,' 'God willing,' or 'Let's hope God hears you' and that's from people who do not consider themselves religious.

Similarly, if someone is paying you or your child a compliment, Bulgarians find it difficult to simply accept the compliment. Instead, they tend to engage in self-criticism. Let's say someone tells an Australian, 'I heard your daughter did really well in her exams.' The Australian will most likely say, 'Thank you, yes, she did,' or 'we are really proud.'

Not a Bulgarian. A Bulgarian parent will say something to the effect of, 'Yes, she did OK, but generally she is lazy' or 'Yes, but she is a disobedient child.' I am not at all sure why I gave this particular example. Surely I am not talking about myself here.

Fatalism aside, Bulgarians have a much greater distrust and suspicion of quiet individuals than Australians do, because they are perceived to be secretive, which in turn is presumed to mean that they have something to hide and hence the proverb 'Still waters are the deepest'. Bulgarians, especially compared with Australians and Anglo-Saxons in general, tend to be loud and blunt, even if they don't think they are. They are emotionally open and expressive, but (and this is a big but), with people they know, not with strangers necessarily.

Do not expect a Bulgarian on the street to crack a smile at a stranger and it is best if you don't do that either. They will either think you are romantically interested in them or you have mental health problems. But once introduced, expect the kind of hospitality you won't find anywhere in the world; they will take you home, feed you, share life stories and write up a travel itinerary for you.

You should also know that a sense of humour and sharing jokes is considered a compulsory part of everyday exchanges in Bulgaria and this is reflected in some of our common proverbs and sayings like: 'A hungry bear does not dance', which really means that a Bulgarian cannot be counted on to do anything on an empty stomach. Bulgarians like their afternoon nap, hence the saying: 'Even a dog needs to have a lie down after he's eaten'.

Most of all, however, Bulgarians appreciate irony. There is no neurosis about placing people and events into neat, two-dimensional boxes; we like imperfection, we like contradictory personalities, we like irony. I am reminded of a famous proverb, which is also a national children's story; it roughly translates to 'The Sick Carry the Healthy' (*Bolen Zdrav Nosi*).

This fairy tale is a typical example of how Bulgarian fairy tales differ from their counterparts in the English language. Fairy tales in the English language generally have a happy ending; the princess marries the prince and they live happily ever after. Good always wins against evil. Bulgarian fairy tales almost always carry a strong current of realism.

Here's the gist of this famous Bulgarian fairy tale, *Bolen Zdrav Nosi*. A sly female fox (Kyma Lisa) sees an old grandpa on his horse with a lot of freshly caught fish in his sleigh. She runs to the middle of the road, collapses and pretends to be dead.

The grandpa stops, picks her up, thinking she will make a great fox coat for his wife. While he is happily riding home, the fox jumps off his sleigh with all his fish, and runs to her little hut in the forest. Her friend, a male wolf (Kymcho Valcho) visits her, and impressed by the large quantity of fish she has, asks her about it. She promptly lies to him that she personally caught it all, and offers to teach him how to fish.

Lady Fox takes him to the river, ties a bucket to his tail and immerses his tail in a hole in the icy river. While the wolf waits for fish, the fox runs to the nearest house, warns the farmer that there is a dangerous wolf outside and while the farmer is outside beating the poor wolf, the fox eats all the farmer's food.

The poor wolf is now missing a tail, badly beaten and hungry. The fox tells him they have been invited to a wedding so the wolf agrees to go. On the way, the fox runs ahead of him, tells the wedding guests there is a dangerous wolf behind her, the guests arm up, chase the wolf and beat him up. Where is the fox in the meantime? She is eating all the wedding food.

When she eventually catches up with the wolf, she lies to him again and tells him that while he has lost a tail, the guests beat her up so badly they cracked her head open and she fears her brain is leaking out. The good old wolf feels so sorry for her, he offers to carry her home on his badly beaten up back.

While the wolf carries the fox, she whispers under her breath, 'the sick is carrying the healthy, the sick is carrying the healthy.' When the wolf makes it to the fox's hut, she bolts off his back, runs inside, locks herself in and tells him how stupid he's been. He, the sick one has been carrying her, the healthy one.

Now at this point you as a reader, start hoping and expecting (given that this is a fairy tale) to see the fox get what she deserves. Furthermore, seeing her punished would be a good lesson for the young reader who is learning about right and wrong. Well, the ending of this story made for some interesting explaining on my part, to my four-year-old, who wanted to know exactly how the fox was punished.

This is the ending. The wolf is angry, he feels betrayed. He starts digging up a hole outside the fox's hut. He manages to get deep enough and underneath so he can catch her foot, and starts pulling on it, but the fox tells him he has got a tree root and laughs at him. The wolf, yet again (so definitely character consistency here) believes the fox, lets go, keeps digging and when he really does have a tree root, the fox lies to him that he has her foot, screams, and he keeps on angrily pulling, until all of a sudden he falls in the deep hole underground and disappears. The End.

Not only does the fox go unpunished, the poor wolf doesn't even get to go home and lick his wounds; he disappears deep underground. Even if he is not dead, chances are, he is not doing well. The moral of the story is that you cannot afford to be naive and stupid in life or you will always suffer, or never offer people a piggy back ride and never trust foxes.

Putting that particular fairy tale aside, the Bulgarian child's imagination is developed early on by exposure to widely different styles of literature from your usual *Cinderella*, *Alice in Wonderland* and *Little Red Riding Hood* to Bulgarian folklore fairy tales, Bulgarian legends, and traditional short stories set in Bulgarian mountains (which tend to develop a love of Bulgarian nature and the mountains early on).

But what is particularly great about growing up in Bulgaria is the access, not only to Bulgarian classics, but classics from around the world. Upcoming writers, as well as prominent writers supplemented their income by translating important literature from various languages, and the culture of learning at least one other foreign language, often more, meant that ordinary Bulgarians had the most magnificent gift at their disposal, and cheaply—perfect translations of important foreign literature.

Bulgarian kids of my era were particularly fond of Hans Christian Anderson's fairy tales, Russian and French fairy tales (which came with amazing brightly coloured and glossy illustrations), German fairy tales by the brothers Grimm, Middle Eastern fairy tales and Scandinavian stories, as well as commonly known English language ones.

As a Bulgarian child myself, my favourite Bulgarian authors were Elin Pelin and Angel Karaliichev. Elin Pelin (real name Dimitar Stoyanov 1877–1949) is widely regarded as Bulgaria's greatest village life or country life narrator, as well as a master of Bulgarian prose. I only know him as a children's writer from his famous work, *Yan Bibian*, about the main character's journey to the moon, but I am aiming to re-familiarise myself with Elin Pelin by reading his equally famous adult works, *Earth* (*Zemia*, published in 1911) and *The Gerak Family* (*Geratsite*, 1922). Clearly, he wrote well before the emergence of socialism in Bulgaria (1944–1946) but he was widely read during Bulgaria's socialist era and the socialist leadership even labelled his works socialist realism.

I am also happy to report that at the end of Angel Karaliichev's Wikipedia profile, in external links, there is a link to an English translation of his fairy tale, *This Pretty Land of Bulgaria*, which concisely explains why Bulgaria is a piece of heaven.

I have tried to introduce my Australian friends to Bulgarian literature but the truth is, it is impossible to find Bulgarian literature translated in English in Australian bookshops. I was pleasantly surprised to discover that the second floor of the Reid Library at the University of Western Australia houses a small section of translated Bulgarian works.

I cannot help but think that had modern day Bulgaria been a bigger country, our most famous writers and poets would be read by the tens of millions outside of their native Bulgaria. The authors and poets I would like to introduce to you are Ivan Vazov (1850–1921), Hristo Botev (1848–1876), Peyo Yavorov (1878–1914), Pencho Slaveikov (1866–1912), Petko Slaveikov (1827–1895), Dimcho Debelianov (1887–1916), Nikola Vaptsarov (1909-1942), Emilian Stanev (1907–1979), Geo Milev (1895–1925), Yordan

Radichkov (1929–2004), Nikolai Haitov (1919–2002), Valery Petrov (1920–2014), Stefan Tsanev and Nedyalko Yordanov, just to mention a few.

I was deliriously excited to find out that one of our most famous historical novels by the above mentioned Ivan Vazov, called *Under the Yoke*, has indeed been translated into English (and approximately 30 other languages as well) and it is available on Amazon. Yes, in Australia you may only buy Bulgarian books via online shopping. I suggest you get online and buy it, because you will be reading a masterpiece and because it is indeed a world classic.

My friend Louisa has already been given this Bulgarian classic for her birthday; I am popularising Bulgarian literature one person at a time. However, I should point out that since this work of art was written in 1888, it deals with that Bulgaria, which has been wiped off the map and written off as a part of the Ottoman Empire. More precisely, the book focuses on the Bulgarian uprising against Ottoman rule, which subsequently led to the Russo–Turkish war, and Bulgaria's independence after 500 years under the rule of the Ottoman Empire. It is therefore a heavy read, but you will not be able to put it down.

Another interesting fact is that an American adaptation of this Bulgarian classic was filmed and directed by J Gordon Edwards in 1918 and produced by a William Fox and distributed by Fox, starring Theda Bara, but like many other silent movies of that era, the film is considered a 'lost film'.

A second happy announcement I would like to make is a most exciting internet discovery—a website I found recently, dedicated to translating Bulgarian poetry and short stories from Bulgarian to various foreign languages, among them English, French, Dutch, Spanish, Greek and Russian. It may not be a hardcover book you can find at Dymocks, but a website can reach millions in this day and age. The website I am rather excited about is www.slovo.bg and to go straight to the section which has been translated into English it is **www.slovo.bg/old/f/en/index.htm**.

My favourite to-read on the list of translated works would be Petya Dubarova, Chudomir, Nikola Vaptsarov and Hristo Botev and the already discussed Ivan Vazov. Under www.slovo.bg/international.php3 click on 'English' and choose, near the bottom of the list of authors, Ivan Vazov. There you will find another one of his most famous works, 'Epic of the Forgotten', a poetic saga (it is about 40 pages long), which is divided into 12 epic poems commemorating and dedicated to some of our most notable national heroes. The site provides a translation of four of the 12 poems—'*Levski*', '*Paissy*', '*Kocho*' and 'The Volunteers at Shipka'.

Slovo also provides a brief one paragraph biographical summary of each author so that the reader is not completely ignorant of the times and historical context of these works of art.

You will notice that the Bulgarian authors mentioned above come from different eras of our history (and are not usually mentioned in the same sentence), and therefore you will get a taste of that which is the essence of the Bulgarian soul across the ages and in spite of the different political ideologies that have been embraced or imposed on Bulgaria through its long and illustrious history.

For example, Hristo Botev, one of our greatest revolutionaries and a poet, was born in 1848 and died in 1876, fighting for Bulgaria's independence from the Ottoman Empire. Next on the list of translated authors at slovo.bg is Nikola Vaptsarov, probably one of our most prominent proletarian poets. He was born in 1909 and shot in 1942, executed for underground activities against the government of Tsar Boris III. Needless to say, given his times, he has poems entitled 'The Comrade's Song', 'The Factory', 'Faith' and 'I Have a Fatherland'.

It is important to note that Nikola Vaptsarov was born when Bulgaria was ruled by a Tsar and died when the country was on the cusp of adopting the Soviet Union model of communism, just a few short years later. His works are therefore, more a reflection of the injustice he felt during the tsarist days and they illustrate the high hopes many had for the socialist ideals and way of life (before those ideals were put into practice). Do not be put off by the word 'communism' because his poetry is above and beyond any political ideology; it is about life. In his poem 'Faith' from his collection *Songs of Man* he says:

But look, suppose
You took—how much?—
A single grain
From this my faith,
Then would I rage
I would rage from pain
Like a panther
Pierced to the heart.

In fact, Nikola Vaptsarov's *Selected Poems* were published in London in 1954 by Lawrence and Wisshart, translated into English with a foreword by the prominent British poet Peter Tempest. It should be noted Vaptsarov's poetry has been translated into 98 languages. Yes, you read correctly—98 languages.

Interestingly, Peter Tempest, I recently discovered, has managed to translate 600 pages worth of famous Bulgarian poems into English, over the course of 30 years. The enormous service he has done to my country is collected in a single book, *Anthology of Bulgarian Poetry*, which I have heard can be ordered on Amazon.

If you Google blazingbulgaria.wordpress.com you will be able to read a short but informative story about Bulgarian literature and publishing. I simply must repeat just how enormous Peter Tempest's contribution is, 600 pages and 30 years of dedicated translation of not one but many of our greatest poets. Bear in mind how nearly impossible it is to translate poetry in particular. Peter Tempest is also listed as the translator of the famous 'September' poem by Geo Milev, which you may read right now if you Google 'Geo Milev, September'.

'September' is probably Geo Milev's most famous poem, and he was murdered, strangled and buried in a mass grave near Sofia, by fascist police only months after he had written the poem and indeed, he was killed because of this poem, which exposes fascist brutality in the most powerful manner. He was just 30 years of age and his fate was unknown for another 30 years, until the trial of various military executioners, who confessed to the 1925 purges and specified the location of the mass grave of the victims. Geo Milev's skull was found and identified because of his glass eye; he had lost an eye in World War I.

Personally, what I have always found most revealing and touching about the Bulgarian character is the way intellectuals unite with their fellow countrymen. There is an absence of a great divide or intellectual snobbery often found in other cultures. Consider Geo Milev, who was one such intellectual. He studied in Leipzig, wrote a thesis on German Expressionism, and then in addition to writing, dedicated himself to publishing, editing, translating and reviewing.

In his introduction to his translation of Geo Milev's poem, Peter Tempest notes a number of Geo Milev quotes, which perfectly illustrate the poet's unity with his countrymen, peasants and workers alike. As Peter Tempest explains, Milev could easily have been the gifted poet who strolled the beautiful parks of Sofia or spent hours at coffee shops philosophising about life, but instead, he found the real patriots of his country to be 'the common folk, landless, illiterate, boors.' He wrote: 'We shall stand where the People are: with the People, among the People' and elaborated that 'The ivory tower, the refuge of poetry and hiding place of poets, lies crumbled in ruins. From the dust of dreams, from the ruin of fantasies, the poet emerges—stunned, astounded, no longer blind—and confronts the blood stained faces of the people, his people ...'

In spite the tragic times he lived in, or perhaps because of the weight of tragedy, words meant so much more than they do today. Thinking of those days when poems were smuggled out of the country, published in foreign countries, then copied and recopied and passed along from person to person, inspires nostalgic feelings in me.

On a brighter note, I must mention that Bulgaria has given the world some romantic poets too. I recommend Petya Dubarova's poetry, some of which may be found at slovo.bg, particularly her collection of poems titled *The Sea and Me*. Her poetry has decidedly romantic undercurrents and it touches on subjects such as love, youth, the Black Sea. Perhaps this is because she lived in an era of peace, having been born in 1962 when Bulgaria had been a socialist state for nearly two decades, and of course, because she was a young poet, her talent having been recognised before she reached ten years of age. Her poems carry titles such as 'Saturdays', 'Mood' and 'Winter Holidays' and talk about the rainbows that fill her eyes and the sky that lives within her and the thousands of rivers running towards her. By the time she turned 12 years of age, Dubarova's poems were accepted for publication in literary journals for adults.

Bear in mind all this was written by a teenager. Petya Dubarova died a tragic death at only 17 years of age when she committed suicide in 1979, shortly after she was accused of an act of vandalism. She had been accused of somehow obstructing the gears of a conveyer belt at a state brewery where she was doing compulsory student volunteer work and it was believed that several teachers (presumed to be envious of the special treatment she enjoyed and her rapid success in the literary world or simply because they believed in punishing student disobedience) conspired to have her punished so severely that she could not bear the injustice.

As a teenager I was more obsessed with reading her diary, which was published in a large volume along with her essays and poems, than her poems. You see, she is not only from my favourite city, Burgas, but from my suburb, the centre of the city, and her diary is full of details of her daily adventures on the very streets, parks and the beach I was to call my backyard 10 years after she wrote about them.

Her summers directly mirrored mine a decade later. She writes of daily visits to the Sea Gardens, Luna Park, the beach, the nightly walks by the sea, followed by dinner at a restaurant with her parents. Several times a week she went to a popular cinema we all went to, and the theatre, she played the guitar (OK, I don't play the guitar but I like people who can play the guitar). She even cites favourite songs which were still played when I was a teenager more than 10 years later, like Gianni Morandi's 'Parla piu piano' (I suggest you listen to this song right now). I recently found her book of letters and her diary in a second-hand bookshop in Burgas and am re-reading it now.

Finally, on the list of translated authors I recommend Chudomir, a writer and a painter who was born in 1890 and died in 1967, having fought in the Balkan wars and in World War I. He too, was born in what was known as the Bulgarian Kingdom but died in what became the People's Republic of Bulgaria. His short stories I still read when I want to feel connected to my great-grandmother's era, dreaming of what appears to be the idyllic country life in Bulgarian villages, but which in reality still carry the same amount of hardship you would find in a Chekov play, just as subtly written between the lines.

Even a light-hearted introduction to Bulgarian literature cannot afford to be short when the list of worthy authors is extensive. I have no choice but to introduce the reader to at least some of the more prominent Bulgarian authors from our illustrious history. I recently found and bought on the internet a great old Bulgarian classic, which is, in fact, a serious study, but written in a light and humorous manner, called *Bai Ganyo: Incredible Tales of a Modern Bulgarian* by Aleko Konstantinov.

Again, in an attempt to popularise Bulgarian literature with my Australian friends, my good friend Kirsty was presented with a copy of *Bai Ganyo* for Christmas. It was translated by a group of North American specialists in Balkan linguistics—Victor Friedman, Christina Kramer, Grace Fielder and Catherine Rudin.

Apparently, a Bulgarian lady by the name of Daniela Hristova, then working at the University of Chicago, informed Victor Friedman that the Bulgarian Aleko Konstantinov Foundation was planning to sponsor the publication of an English translation of *Bai Ganyo* and this is how this 1895 novel came to life in the English language in 2002. Students at the University of Chicago apparently consider this book the highlight of their Bulgarian studies. For more information on obtaining a copy visit uwpress.wisc.edu or eurospanbookstore.com.

Bai Ganyo is a merchant of peasant origin who demonstrates his crudeness and vulgarity wherever he goes, from Russia, Switzerland and Germany to the Austro-Hungarian Empire. It is important to note that the author of this work, Aleko Konstantinov, was the complete opposite of his hero, Bai Ganyo—he was refined, educated and a lawyer before embarking on a writing career, and he was extremely well-travelled around Europe and America.

Another famous Bulgarian author who is a favourite and a Bulgarian literary legend is Yordan Yovkov. Yordan Yovkov, coincidently, did not appreciate Aleko Konstantinov's *Bai Ganyo* because it angered him to see the Bulgarian peasant portrayed as uncivilised. Yovkov had a deep respect for Bulgarian peasants and his short stories, written in the 1920s, were focused on this section of society. His famous collection of short stories is called *The Legends of Stara Planina*, which means The Legends of Stara Mountain. For him, the essence of the Bulgarian soul and what is good about Bulgaria is to be found amongst the hard-working peasants. I am proud to inform you that one of his stories, *The Sin of Ivan Belin* is included in Thomas Mann's 1956 anthology *The Most Beautiful Stories in the World*.

Bulgaria's most significant writer of the last third of the 20th century is Yordan Radichkov (1929–2004), and for those of you who are familiar with 19th-century Russian literature, Radichkov is often also referred to as the Bulgarian Gogol. His style of writing is a mixture of fantasy, folklore and realism, which has been labelled Balkan Magic Realism; a label I find strangely appealing.

As a young girl, I was mostly familiar with his children's literature rather than his serious adult works, but having read about him recently, I am going to dig deeper and immerse myself into his works, particularly the new edition of his short stories *Svirepo Nastroenie* (Ferocious Mood). He was nominated for a Nobel Prize in literature twice, the second time as recently as 2001, and has been awarded various prestigious Italian, French and Swedish, as well as Bulgarian awards for literature.

At school Radichkov, by his own admission, was a poor student in literature in particular. He states that a D was his usual mark (in Bulgaria a three) because he could never write in the conventionally accepted format with a clear introduction, a body and a conclusion, and he never did. I have always loved stories that show a clear and overwhelming example of one individual proving any organised, accepted system wrong.

Unfortunately, although Radichkov has been translated into 30 languages, it is still difficult to find many translated works in the English language. I have been able to find only one short story translated into English, *Container*, available at culture360.asef. org. His best children's books (sometimes illustrated with his own abstract sketches) are *The Little Frogs' Stories* (*Malki Jabeshki Istorii*) and *We, The Sparrows* (*Nie Vrabchetata*) and his most prominent works for adults are *The Last Summer* (*Posledno Liato*, 1974) and *Gunpowder Primer* (*Baryten Bukvar*, 1969).

I am reluctant to tell you that I recently read an old interview with this most distinguished writer and when asked, 'Where shall we look for the spirit, the Bulgarian spirit?', Radichkov said, 'It is often mentioned but I gather that whoever mentions it is hardly aware of what they mean.' So much for my efforts to introduce you to the Bulgarian spirit.

A contemporary Bulgarian writer I am desperate to see translated into English is Stefan Tsanev. In particular, his volumes entitled *Bulgarian Chronicles*. These books will make you wish you were born Bulgarian, and if you are in fact Bulgarian, you will be unable to finish these volumes, because on every page there is something that will make you so proud to be Bulgarian you will find yourself wanting to call everyone you know to tell them about this great Bulgaria, and you will find yourself so excited, your nerves will not allow you to continue reading.

Similarly, when things do not go the Bulgarian's way and tragedy strikes, (as has happened many a time in Bulgarian history) again, you will find a tremendous anger build up and you will be unable to keep going. So far I have been unable to both maintain my emotional stability and read these awe-inspiring literary books at the same time. But I will one day. I have, however, read his diary from the period 1978–2002, which I will be mentioning later.

In terms of poetry, the famous poet and Nobel Prize nominee, Valery Petrov, is particularly interesting to me, firstly and rather obviously for his poetry (which is so endearing, and refined you feel as though this most gentle soul is speaking to you his words of infinite wisdom ever so softly) but also because he lived through the most interesting times.

Valery Petrov was born in 1920 in what was The Third Bulgarian Kingdom, worked in socialist Bulgaria and continues to live (now in his 90s) in this time, which we no longer know what to call. Valeri Petrov is responsible for a highly esteemed translation of Shakespeare's entire body of work into Bulgarian in the early 1970s. Coincidently, the 1970s was the period when he clashed with the communist regime, because he refused to sign a petition denouncing the Nobel Prize award of the Soviet dissident Alexander Solzhenitsyn. Consequently, his own works were not published for a number of years, during which time he turned to translating. He is someone whose memoir I would love to read but I suspect his modesty would prevent him from writing a memoir.

I have listed mostly my personal favourites of the classic authors, and there are many I myself have not yet studied. But this will be corrected in the years to come and annually as I make my way back to Bulgaria. I will be re-reading *Pet Prikazki* (*Five Fairy Tales*) by Valery Petrov (1986) and *Divi Razkazi* (*Wild Stories*) by Nikolai Haitov (1967) as soon as possible.

Ideally, I would also immerse myself in some Balkan Magic Realism with Yordan Radichkov and discover the great romantic poetry of Hristo Fotev. Late at night, when everyone is asleep, and when I too, should be sleeping, I like to read Dimcho Debelianov's poems. He has been labelled Bulgaria's most gentle of poets.

I can assure you without any reservation that whomever you choose to read from my recommended authors, will enrich your inner world in ways you could not possibly anticipate.

CHAPTER ELEVEN

Return to Bulgaria and the beginning of Australian university life

B y the time I returned to Bulgaria at the end of 1996, just before I was due to start first year of university in Australia, I had seen so many white picket fences, one storey houses and buildings and so much space, I was craving the energy of Bulgaria and Europe in general.

I craved that energy you feel when you find yourself in a congested area with people from all walks of life and all age groups on display right in front of you, on streets that seem to pop up out of all possible directions. When there are cars, buses, trolley buses and taxis buzzing by, loud talking, the smell of cigarette smoke, men in track pants and gold chains, women in sophisticated suits, old ladies in fur coats and hats. That had not changed in the three years that I had been in Australia—women were still elegantly dressed—but some things had changed, at least, according to my parents. When we arrived back in Sofia in 1996, my parents were shocked at how dirty the city had become, how the roads were no longer maintained and that there was graffiti in all sorts of places you wouldn't imagine.

Strange as it sounds, none of these rather obvious changes affected me or even registered in my mind. My 18-year-old self was so thrilled to be back; I was too busy floating on Bulgarian air. Australia had been so tidy and ordered, and life felt so linear, I craved and readily welcomed some chaos.

The only thing that made an impression was the sight of homeless people. I had seen homeless people in Paris and in London but never in Bulgaria. And now we had homeless people in Bulgaria and the million dollar Mercedes which was supposed to be quite rare around the rest of the world, but was in high supply in the centre of Sofia.

I could not deny that some things had changed in three years. There was a particular highly-charged energy that could be felt across the country, and that was foreign to me, because it was so distinctly different from the way Bulgaria felt to me growing up in the 1980s. The only way I could describe it would be to say that there was a definitive feeling of intensity and uncertainty, yet simultaneously, I could sense an uneasy excitement pulsating through the streets. Strangers on the streets seemed to radiate an air of frustration, short temper, even rudeness, and their discussions were highly charged and animated.

There was a sense the country and its people were on a mission, a fast-paced race toward something, and it felt exciting to be there. Fortunately, enough of what I loved about Bulgaria had remained unchanged, and it is precisely that that I chose to see and experience again. And that is what I continue to do every year to this day. I have chosen my reality and I shall remain loyal to it.

I stayed at my cousin's apartment because I wouldn't dream of going home alone when I could spend the night with family, gathered around the kitchen table, talking late into the night. Late at night, I stepped outside to throw out some rubbish in the bin on the balcony and what I saw excited me to no end. Across from my cousin's apartment, past a children's playground, there was another apartment block, and from my cousin's balcony I could see a fat middle-aged man smoking a cigarette in his underwear on his balcony (in spite the cold weather). Next to the underwear smoker, I could see a woman cooking, and on the floor below them I could see a man and a woman watching TV in their living room, not having pulled their curtains yet. I could also hear bits and pieces of at least two different conversations going on either below my cousin's balcony or above.

I was so excited to see and hear these strangers going on about their life. This was the Bulgarian vibe I was longing for. If I were to meet these people I probably would not find them remotely exciting, but standing there, on my cousin's balcony, being allowed to watch these strangers go about their life, I was thrilled. I had been allowed to witness something personal, even if it was a banal and trivial part of their life, and I felt connected to these strangers without even having to interact with them.

In Australia, looking out the window always feels like I am on holiday somewhere exotic but remote, where I can have my needed solitude, where there is always a beautiful silence, but just a little too much silence. After a while, the silence gets too much to take and there is only so much solitude I need. I see the front yard of my next-door neighbours but I don't catch a glimpse of them. I don't hear them. I don't feel connected to them.

I often miss the feeling I always seem to get when in Bulgaria, that I am right in the middle of where life is taking place and that I am a part of the universe. I feel exhilarated. Of course, after a while in Europe I start to crave the Australian peace and silence, that extra bit of space between you and your neighbours. That's the problem with having a life in two countries—you always miss something wherever you are. But having a home in more than one country, a home with things in it that tell a story about your life in that particular place, that grounds me; solidifies my sense of belonging there. It makes my life feel more dynamic, more diverse, more fulfilling, richer. It is also beyond exciting to have friends from one country visit your 'other country' and see you in your other habitat.

Upon my return from Bulgaria and shortly before I started university at 18 years of age, or 18.5 to be precise, I had decided that socialising with fellow Europeans, rather than completely immersing myself in Australian culture, was not conducive to happiness and joy. Because I intended to return to Bulgaria full time, I started to feel that my time in Australia was limited and to return to Europe without having experienced Australian culture was something I would live to regret.

The decision to immerse myself in all things Australian was reached after the realisation that I had incorrectly assumed that I had a lot in common with the Eastern Europeans I had met in Perth. With time, I began to appreciate that our experiences, both in Australia and in Europe, were qualitatively different. Yes, the three or four people I have in mind were homesick, just like I was, but their homesickness had an added dimension of sadness and fatalism absent from my childlike experience of homesickness. While I missed my family and friends and felt depressed about the fact that I had missed several Christmas celebrations at home and my school ball in Bulgaria, I did not appreciate the fact that I could always return home, not just to Bulgaria, but to my actual home, my own bed, my own room, and all my material possessions, books, clothes and all the things that make you feel grounded in a particular place.

In contrast, these people did not live with an enduring shadow of homesickness, they lived with the knowledge that it would be some years before they were able to return to their home countries and when they did, they would not have their childhood homes or anything material that allowed them to feel like they still belonged there. Yet at the same time, they could not possibly feel at home in a country as great as Australia is, where they are still foreigners, adjusting to a foreign language and foreign customs.

It must be difficult to derive a sense of optimism about the near future when you also consider the pain and disappointment of their parents, who had found themselves unemployed in their own country and underappreciated (at least at the beginning) in their adopted country. I, as a young girl not yet out of my teen years, could not appreciate any of these factors and simply felt depressed listening to negative commentary about Australia. I also found myself a touch protective of Australia; I could privately complain about Australia all I liked but I was not happy to hear others complain about it. Therefore, I made the decision to only socialise with Australians and to fully immerse myself in Australian culture.

The decision to change my social circle (which was not large to begin with) from mostly Eastern and Southern Europeans to 'Aussie' Australians presented new challenges. Australians are known for being warm and friendly and that starts at a young age. However, they have slightly different social habits from the ones I was used to.

For example, a typical weekend get-together in Perth for young boys and girls in the 1990s involved the following—the parents drive their children to a big shopping centre, which houses many shops, a cinema and fast food restaurants. The kids then meet their friends inside and several hours later, after a movie, shopping and eating (all indoors in a big closed-off institution of a place) return to the car park like a pack of well-behaved monkeys to be picked up by their parents.

To this day, more than 15 years later, I cannot think of a less romantic place than a shopping mall. This Australian teenage ritual was a problem for me on several levels. Firstly, the necessity of having to involve my parents in my social life by having them drive me to see my friends horrified me. It defeated any minute sense of independence I felt I had. Then the idea of spending several hours voluntarily closed off in an air-conditioned institution-like environment, designed exclusively to force me to spend all the limited amount of pocket money I had, just because there was nothing else to do, did not inspire me in the slightest. As a result, I often found myself at home reading books, which led my parents to believe that I was not adjusting well to life in Perth. That, and some of my 'poetry' from those years.

What is school?
It is a carefully calculated
Fucked up system.
And the purpose?
Explicitly—to teach you
Implicitly—to make you suffer in order to prepare you for life
But in the process they sacrifice your spirit
The way out?
No way out.
Or
There is so much I do not understand
So much I do not know
So much I need to know
So much I will never know
But so much is gone
In so little time
A fraction of a second
When all the right words
And all the right intentions
Have no impact
Mean so little
Do not matter

I found teenagers in Australia exceedingly obedient. Not a single person I knew wished to skip class. It was truly depressing. It was not a fear of the consequences; they simply had no desire to skip class and they did not know what to do with themselves or where to go if they did.

But why would they? There was no need of a resistance movement. There was nothing to oppose or resist. They lived in households where they were told to have fun and enjoy themselves. Parents were careful never to push them too hard, teachers were careful not to do anything that may lower their self-esteem. They were allowed just about everything they desired and their parents were their personal taxi drivers, driving them to whatever it is they desired, the many extracurricular activities designed to enhance their self-discovery and boost their self-esteem.

Sure, there were drugs, but that's something you heard about on TV. I never met anyone who was a drug user, or at least, I was never aware of it. I still refer to marijuana as marijuana, so draw your conclusions from that detail alone.

Yes, I am as innocent as they come (maybe that is why mother nature is shaking things up and decided to bless me with three sons). My rebellion was exclusively focused on asserting a sense of freedom and independence from strict parents; that is all. I wanted to skip class, go for a walk, then sit at a café and talk about life and books. I did not get to do that in high school in Perth, hence the moody poetry.

My social life in Bulgaria was, I felt, vastly different. Whether I was in Sofia (during school term) or in Burgas (during the holidays), socialising with friends involved walking myself (minus parents) and/or catching a tram, a trolley bus or a bus to a central public place—a building, a statue or a park—the designated meeting place. From there, while enjoying a diverse range of architecture, fresh air (not air-conditioning) and a lot of people watching, we would then walk to a second location of interest, picking up all sorts of snacks—Bulgarian pastry (*banichka*), pretzels, cappuccino (popular with teenagers in 1991–1992), or we would stop for cake somewhere and even smoke a cigarette (OK, that only happened a few times when I was 13).

We would spend hours exploring the city, enjoying public spaces, benches, bookstores, cafés and the movies. When we went to the movies, the entrance to the cinema was from a street, next to all sorts of shops and cafés, rather than inside a shopping mall surrounded by a large car park. The feeling was different even if the activity (eating, seeing a movie) was the same.

One of my favourite activities while out and about was looking for books. Books, to me, contain the secrets of life and I attributed almost magical qualities to the book shopping experience. I could not imagine anything more exciting or romantic than searching through a pile of books to find the special one, always believing that it was the book that chose me rather than the other way around.

And book shopping at night, oh, it tips me over the edge with excitement. In Sofia there is a street in the centre of the city, *Graf Ignatiev* Street, at Slaveikov Square, which is lined up with book stalls (it is an open market for books) on both sides of the street, with trams running in the middle. You can spend hours looking at books and gossiping with your companions along the way, while people are watching and overhearing the conversations of people from all age groups and walks of life. You would see ladies in fur coats walking past skinheads.

In Burgas one of my favourite second-hand bookshops is on a street called Bogoridi, which is located in the centre of the city, and it leads straight to the Sea Gardens (one of my most favourite places in the world), which overlook the Black Sea. The layout of the city is such that the centre of the city joins the Sea Gardens in the direction of the beach. Given that my entire family lives right in the centre of Burgas, the beach, the Sea Gardens and the glorious pedestrian streets full of shops and cafés and restaurants, as well as the train station and all administrative buildings comprise my suburb, are my backyard and my front yard.

Imagine taking a casual walk to the bookstore, walking past cafés, smelling various freshly cooked Bulgarian delights, and then, after you have found yourself a fabulously smelling old book which will reveal to you all sorts of exciting life stories, you find yourself in this magical garden surrounded by flowers and trees, overlooking the Black Sea. Scattered all around you, between flowers and trees, stand statues and sculptures. The Burgas Sea Gardens is home to 36 statues of famous Bulgarian artists, poets, soldiers and revolutionaries, and 86 sculptures, including another 15 which do not have a sign. The Bulgarian Stefan Apostolov has written a book detailing the history of the entire Burgas region and he has managed to reference the precise number of statues and sculptures in the city's famous Sea Gardens.

In Sofia my favourite park is *Borisova Gradina*. It is one of the oldest parks in Sofia (its arrangement began in the late 1880s) and it is named after our last tsar, Tsar Boris III. I still do not understand how it is that tourists are never advised to visit this vast greenery in the centre of the city, all 300,000 square metres of it, with endless statues and flowerbeds, tennis courts, a swimming pool, a massive football stadium, and Lake Ariana, where you will find my favourite traditional Bulgarian restaurant, *Edno Vreme* (Once Upon a Time). Putin and Metallica have dined there and since it is one of my most favourite restaurants in the city, I highly recommend you too, enjoy an exquisite Bulgarian lunch there, with a table outside directly on the lake. Please make sure you try a traditional Bulgarian salad from their extensive list, the homemade platter for two (with various dips, special bread and marinated grilled vegetables) and the chicken *sach* on a hot plate (pronounced 'such').

After all that food you will need a romantic walk and I recommend you simply walk across the little bridge outside the restaurant to cross straight into the glory of the park, *Borisova Gradina*. I still remember this park by its name from the socialist era, *Park na Svobodata* or Freedom Park. It reverted back to its original name sometime after 1989 but you can still see the 42m high Soviet monument, called Mount of Brotherhood. This would be an example of socialist realism, I imagine. I am yet to learn the difference between socialist realism and Stalinist gothic.

Speaking of my favourite park in Sofia, I am now eager to advise you on Sofia's most beautiful walks, as determined by my distinctly romantic tastes. There are a thousand different walks you could go on to see my favourite places in Sofia, but why don't we start with The National Library, St Cyril and Methodius (in Bulgarian Kiril I Metodii) on Vasil Levski Boulevard. Begin the day with a coffee at the romantic, glass domed café immediately behind the library, then walk around the library, take a moment to remind yourself that you are indeed in this unique city and enjoy the view of the bright terracotta-coloured National Academy of Arts, directly opposite the library.

Continue down the street to reach the main building of Sofia's oldest university, St Kliment Ohridski, and enjoy its exquisite Baroque beauty, before you cross the street to reach the famous boulevard, Tsar Osvoboditel. Between Tsar Osvoboditel and my favourite street, Shipka, you will find the National Assembly Square and the rather grand equestrian statue of Alexander II of Russia or Monument to the Liberators.

Locate Shipka Street and feel the romance as you walk past the elegant pink mansion that houses the Austrian Embassy at four Shipka Street. Stop and enter the lobby of the hotel directly across the street from the embassy, Sense Hotel, at 16 Tsar Osvoboditel Boulevard, and go straight to the rooftop bar on level nine for the magical panoramic view of the city centre.

Then continue on Tsar Osvoboditel Boulevard, past the regal Central Military Club (which now houses the very posh Black Label Whisky Bar) to reach the exquisite Russian Church, St Nicholas. After a quiet moment inside this magical little place, stop and enjoy your surroundings in the little garden next to the church, from where you will see one of my favourite buildings in all of Sofia, purely for its most beautiful roof with a statue of a mother with two children looking down on St Nicholas Church.

Continue on my favourite boulevard and you will reach Alexander Battenberg Square, which houses the National Art Gallery inside the former royal palace. Following a tour of the gallery, make your way directly opposite the gallery and you will find yourself in Sofia City Garden. Here you will enjoy people-watching, young and old strangers playing chess, some accordion playing, and when you spot an elegant fountain with a statue of a petite naked girl striking a graceful ballet-like pose you will know you are standing in front of the National Theatre, Ivan Vazov, and its full Neoclassical splendour.

Explore the little streets all around the theatre, enjoy a nice meal, and get ready to walk back to Alexander Battenberg Square. This time, continue on in the direction of downtown Sofia until you reach the imposing Stalinist-Gothic Party House. Walk all around the Party House and you will encounter not only the Presidency Building, the Sheraton Hotel, the famous department store TSUM and the Rotunda of St George but ancient ruins of the Thracian and Roman city of Serdica at Sofia Largo.

Allow plenty of time to immerse yourself in several millennia worth of history and then make your way back to the area behind the Party House and locate another one of my favourite streets, Moskovska. Here, on Moskovska 6A, you will find The Tobacco Garden Bar at the back of the former royal palace. In fact, the private garden of the bar belonged to the royal palace in our tsarist days.

Following a nice romantic break on Moskovska Street, continue your walk down to Oborishte and you will find yourself at the Balkan's most exquisite and grand cathedral, Alexander Nevsky Cathedral. Do not be satisfied enjoying only the exterior of the cathedral with its grand Neo-Byzantine style and the imposing gold-plated domes. Be sure to visit the cathedral and view not only the exquisite icons but the mosaics shipped from Venice, the Italian marble of various colours and the Brazilian onyx, and the unique Bulgarian calming atmosphere.

From there, enjoy a short walk around until you secure the services of a taxi to take you straight to St Nedelia Church. Enjoy your brief taxi break because you are about to walk straight up from the church the entire length of our famous Boulevard Vitosha or as we say, Vitoshka, all the way past cafés, exclusive shops, and the glorious Sofia trams to reach the immense National Palace of Culture (more than 10,000 tonnes of steel were used for its construction, which is 3000 tons more than the Eiffel Tower). By the time you reach the National Palace of Culture, you should be ready for dinner or at least a drink, and that you can enjoy from the rooftop restaurant of the National Palace of Culture, Sky Plaza.

This is what I love about Bulgaria. You can be spontaneous, because you can engage in all of your favourite activities in one outing. You can shop for books on your way to the park and sit at a café or dine out at the same time as encountering a cross-section of society and a wide variety of architecture from different millennia. And I do mean different millennia; you could walk out of a hotel in the centre of Sofia and trip over ancient ruins, and when you look up you might be facing a Baroque building on one side and a socialist realism statue on the other. This last example may not hold aesthetic value for some but socialist realism monuments and statues were considered art at one time and that would mean they hold historical value (it being a dead art now). That, and I hate to see anything demolished or destroyed. Someone (and I am confident it was not the communist leadership who rolled up their sleeves) must have worked hard to create and build these. To destroy them would be uncivilised.

I have lost my train of thought after this latest diversion, as interesting as it was. I was talking about the depressing level of teenage obedience I encountered in the 1990s in Australia and then somehow I ended up talking about books (I always end up talking about books) and all the romantic book shopping you can enjoy in Bulgaria. This reminds me of another cultural difference. As a young Bulgarian girl in Australia I was also surprised, when visiting Australian friends' homes, to find that just like there is a lot less furniture in an Australian home than in a Bulgarian home (where you cannot move without bumping into floor to ceiling furniture pieces and stepping on Aladdin-like rugs, which I adore), there are Australian homes without a single bookcase in the living room. Some people have a bookcase in their study for work, or study-related books with an occasional hobby book, but there are homes with living rooms without a bookcase.

It is only after visiting a few homes which do not house a bookcase that I discovered I am most comfortable with a living space if there are books and wooden bookcases around me. I am not the only one to make this observation. The anti-communist Russian, Vladimir Bukovsky, makes a similar observation in his book *To Choose Freedom* (1987). He claims that reading is 'far more widespread' in the Soviet Union than it is in England. Vladimir Bukovsky is a Soviet concentration camp survivor who was released by then Soviet leader Brezhnev and let out of the Soviet Union in exchange for a Chilean communist in 1976. He now lives and works in England, and his books and lectures attract worldwide attention.

Having romanticised my Bulgarian walks and book shopping trips, I am reminded again of Jan Morris' impressions of Bulgaria in the early 1990s, recounted in her book, *Europe: An Intimate Journey*. She writes that 'No patriot on earth is more patriotic than a Bulgar and nothing is more symbolic than a Bulgarian symbol.' Jan Morris appears to have been surprised by the sheer number of monuments across the country dedicated to national heroes and poets.

She had travelled the country, glimpsed something of the Bulgarian psyche, and even noted some of our symbols of "pride and defiance", the famous lion statues. I also liked her description of the city of Ruse: 'surprisingly elegant—rather Viennese, with well-proportioned boulevards and lots of sidewalk cafés', just the way I think of my Bulgarian walks.

I realise now that I began this chapter complaining about the Australian teenagers' custom of spending their free time in shopping malls, but that is not entirely true. It is not completely true because the truth is, many Australian teenagers, boys and girls, in just about equal number, were also actively socialising on sports courts, not just at the mall. There was a large portion of the student population who were too over-scheduled to go to the mall because they played sports every afternoon or night of the week from Wednesday to Sunday.

And they like to sweat; the girls too. Sweating is a prerequisite for a good sports session in Australia. This is opposed to my personal philosophy on physical activity—the onset of a drop of sweat is my cue to immediately stop whatever activity is causing it; I am Bulgarian.

Let us consider Bulgarian sportiness versus Australian sportiness for a moment. Australians take their sports more seriously than most Bulgarians I know (except professional athletes). In Bulgaria, being sporty, to me, meant going mountain hiking with my family and relatives. When I say hiking, what I really mean is walking at a leisurely pace, stopping for a picnic, nice food and drink, looking at the scenery, talking, getting fresh mountain air and definitely no sweating involved.

If I were feeling particularly sporty, I'd swap my little navy-blue leather mini-heels for sandals (yes sandals, not running shoes) and play badminton. Some Australians do not seem to realize that badminton is a sport. At my sportiest I played tennis in Sofia and again, I use the term 'played' to describe the hitting of a tennis ball with a tennis racquet, but not necessarily following any rules or even holding the racquet correctly, since I was self-taught. I was self-taught because I did not wish to be told what to do and how to do it; I was already going to school, and also, having to retain and follow rules tends to kill the spontaneity of it all. I was playing for fun, after all. This was the extent of my sportiness.

Many people in Bulgaria choose one sport, usually tennis or soccer, and focus on playing just these on the weekend. In Australia, I was amazed to discover that boys and girls delighted in playing not just one sport weekly, but every sport known to mankind, except it seems, weightlifting, boxing and wrestling. The girls, I discovered, also loved to wear the same kind of t-shirts and shorts as the boys, Billabong and Quicksilver, and the same kind of sunglasses. I would often overhear girls explaining to each other why they could not meet on a particular day, 'Oh, I can't, I have swimming on Wednesday, basketball on Thursday, netball on

Friday and Saturday I coach indoor soccer.' I had not even heard of indoor soccer.

I don't come from an un-sporty nation. At our best Olympics in Moscow 1980, Bulgaria, a country of eight million people, came third in the world, with 41 medals (eight gold, 16 silver and 17 bronze) with 270 athletes in 20 sports and 151 events. Sure, the US (and some others) boycotted those particular Olympics, but that's a minor detail. Then there are sports where Bulgaria consistently performs at the highest level. Our Stefka Kostadinova still holds the women's world record for the high jump (2.09m) she set in 1987. She has 13 gold medals and two silver medals in high jump from the Olympic Games, world championships and European athletics championships.

Then we have our rhythmic gymnasts. Maria Gigova holds four consecutive gold medals in hoop (1967, 1969, 1971, 1973), an achievement still unmatched in gymnastics and for which she is recorded in the *Guinness Book of World Records*. She also holds nine gold medals, two silver and two bronze from world championships between 1967–1973. Maria Petrova shares the world record for the most individual world all-round rhythmic gymnastics titles of all time (with her fellow Bulgarian Maria Gigova and Evgeniya Kanaeva). She has nine gold medals from world championships between 1993 and 1995 and a further six gold medals from European championships between 1992 and 1994 in everything from ball, clubs, ribbon, hoop, all-round and team.

Weightlifting, sumo wrestling, sambo (a type of martial art) and boxing are all sports where Bulgaria can be counted on to bring medals. Yordanka Donkova holds the world record for hurdling (1988). Valentin Yordanov is a seven-time world champion, seven-time European champion and the only sportsman to hold ten medals (seven gold) from world championships in wrestling.

More recently, our men's volleyball team has been doing very well. Then we have chess, and our very own Veselin Topalov, a Bulgarian chess grandmaster who was ranked world number one in 2005–2006, then regained his world number one title in 2008, holding it until 2010. We also have Antoaneta Stefanova, who was the women's world champion for 2004. More recently in 2013, the 16-year-old Denitsa Dragieva became the world champion under 17 years old, and in the same year, Tsvetan Stoyanov won the world championships for kids under nine years old. The Bulgars are a brainy bunch. What other small nation do you know that can be counted on to deliver in so many fields, ranging from academic to sports?

Speaking of sports and the sports gear preferred by young Australians, I am reminded of my own introduction to Australian fashion. In the 1990s, teenage girls in Perth, but also many older women, were dressing in what I would consider exceptionally casual clothes. Women, who were dressed in a manner us Bulgarians would call elegant, were often referred to as yuppies in Australia, and their style seemed to be associated more with their wealth and socio-economic status than with personal style.

I often overheard several Eastern European ladies who had recently moved to Australia, and had started working in Perth, complain to my mother that their clothes were considered too posh and over-dressed in Australian offices, whereas in their respective countries that was considered elegant and sophisticated but certainly not a mark of importance or level of wealth.

My teenage self at the time was also dissatisfied because I felt that my school's dress code did not allow me sufficient self-expression. I would often wear clothing combinations that prompted my Australian classmates (who favoured the school uniform or unisex sports gear) to say, 'You know, a scarf is not a belt. It goes around your neck, not your waist.'

By the time I started university, I was wearing suits to all my first and second-year lectures, and the fact that I was the only one doing so did not seem to discourage me in the slightest. I was starting to resemble my mother, my aunt, my grandmother and a lot of Bulgarian women. It could also have been that after the age of 17, my grandmother presented me with a suit every year on my return to Bulgaria, and often a blazer as well, as a combined Christmas and birthday present. She and my aunt did this for a good five or so years, or until I had accumulated about 11 suits by the time I was 23 or 24.

In Australia, I was often viewed as over-dressed and my good friends saw it as part of my 'Bulgarian charm', or at least that's what I would like to think. When my style relaxed a little after my second year of university, my grandmother was not impressed. Upon noticing that I was about to leave the house in a pair of jeans, even paired with a nice blazer she had bought for me and a scarf, she stopped me to inform me that jeans are OK at home and at the villa if I am planting vegetables or flowers (I have never been trusted to do either of those), as they are 'workman's clothes', but certainly not when going out in public to meet friends.

There also seemed to be a difference, by and large, in the preferred dress code of Australian women working for government organisations versus the private sector, as I discovered when I had to do three placements during my Master's degree at both government and private sector workplaces. A large number of female government employees (obvious generalisation but I did find a noticeable difference between government and private sector employees) not only seemed to feel more comfortable dressing down and wearing a cardigan to work (or leaving one at the office on the back of their chair), they did not seem to like women or girls who dressed in suits.

In contrast, women working for the private sector seemed judgemental and openly looked down on women who dressed casually at the workplace. Where I came from, dressing as elegantly as possible was a sign of self-respect and great taste, but in Australia at that time, it seemed, your dress sense was a sign of status rather than taste. I am also happy to report that these days, in the 2000s, Perth women tend to be elegantly dressed, and very much in touch with European fashion trends.

I have noticed some of the tendencies of Australian men as well. For example, men in Australia seem reluctant to mix and match and experiment with suits. When an Australian male wears a suit, he prefers to stick to a safe black or navy blue and he would never be eager to wear a mismatched top and bottom or a pair of formal pants that are a different colour and/or fabric from their blazer. In Bulgaria you will commonly see men wearing a jacket of one colour and a pair of different colour pants; it is their preferred uniform. They also wear scarves, which is not all that common in Australia.

These days Bulgarian fashion is a little different from my childhood. I still buy most of my clothes in Bulgaria because there is great variety and because we have particularly high-quality fabrics (Bulgaria, unlike many Western European countries, has a discipline and an industry called textile engineering and you can still find amazing fabrics). There is also an immense variety in shoe styles and the best handbags in the world. This statement can be confirmed by my husband and every friend of ours who has visited us in Bulgaria. I get a lot of compliments on my Bulgarian handbags in Australia. But these days there is also a lot of what I call bling-bling fashion, which seems to be popular, particularly with young people.

The Bulgaria of my childhood did not have bling-bling fashion and women of all age groups, including young girls, were extremely well dressed. Do not be fooled by anyone trying to sell you the idea that there was some sort of grey, subdued colour communist uniform worn while strutting with a communist manifesto in hand. You should visit the website www.lostbulgaria.com to catch a glimpse of life in those days. Beyond the elegantly dressed women, something else that will strike you is how clean and orderly the place was, the variety of architecture, how nicely maintained the parks were, the crowded beaches and camping sites across unspoilt nature. You could also see old communist era ads; yes, we had ads for perfume, washing detergent, cars, hotels, cigarettes and alcohol.

The first few years in Australia I stubbornly insisted on wallowing in Bulgarian homesickness, reading books and maintaining friendships with other Europeans. By the time I decided to immerse myself completely in Australian culture, towards the end of high school and just before I started university, I experienced wave upon wave of culture shock.

Forget customs like spending your free time at the mall and playing a multitude of sports (and actively working to achieve a sweat), the way young people enjoyed themselves and felt joy was completely different.

The clearest example I can give to highlight just how out of place someone like me was (or how prissy I may have come across to Australian girls) refers to 1990s nightclubbing. I have never been a serious nightclubbing person, not as a teenager and not in my twenties. I have always had a strong preference for a quiet bar, a nice cocktail (the sweeter the better), followed by five to six glasses of water, space to sit and chat and music that is not so loud as to induce an epileptic fit (I do not suffer from epilepsy, by the way).

If I cannot have a conversation and I have to scream at another person's face while drunken guys are spilling their drinks all over me and bright lights are flickering on and off, I get bored and irritated and I feel the urge to leave. Therefore, my personal clubbing experiences were limited but I was fairly familiar with the Perth clubbing scene, thanks to the hundreds of stories I overheard on the bus to and from university. Just like in Bulgaria, you learn a lot about daily life in a given city when you enjoy the public transport system of that city.

I come from a heavy spirits drinking country. Young Australian males could not keep up with my 87-year-old grandfather. Furthermore, it is a country where girls drink seriously strong drinks but always manage to appear sober and sound sober. They drink, they have fun but they don't drink with getting drunk as the objective.

Knowing how to hold your alcohol is a vital skill in Bulgaria. I know girls in Bulgaria who can simultaneously have shots of vodka and keep a straight face while carrying on a conversation about their PhDs in biology. Some of this may be attributed to genetics; drinking spirits in that part of Europe keeps you warm in winter and has done so for many generations (2012 winter did see several days of -27 C in Sofia), so perhaps we have evolved genetically to have a high level of tolerance for strong spirits (insert wink here).

A lot of it is also cultural; even my great grandmother would have a shot of vodka if she felt the onset of a flu or cold coming on and to this day I am convinced that a few days of drinking a few sips of vodka will fix anything. My great-grandmother never had a cold, lived to 97.5 without ever having been sick or in hospital. Whatever your explanation, I was unprepared for the Australian drinking stories I heard all around me, at the cafeteria and on the bus.

Phrases such as 'and like' and 'you know' were considered an essential part of every sentence produced by an Australian person of the 16–21 age group, sometimes even older. A typical story would go something like this: 'And I got drunk, you know, and like, I threw up all over the side of the street, and oh my God, it was freaking hilarious.' Then a second girl would try to top this amazing drinking story and her story would go something like this: 'Oh my God, wait till you hear this! I was at (insert the name of a popular club/bar) and I was having shots, and like, you know, I chuck all over the bar, you know. And my friends are trying to hold me up, and the bartender's like, get her out of here, and then a bouncer asked us to leave, and I am like, "what the hell?"'

Putting aside the curious linguistic additions of 'you know' and 'like', which seem to make zero contribution to the storytelling, what was most shocking to me was the absence of a sense of humiliation for having thrown up in a public place, in full view of others. There was almost a sense of pride that could be observed.

The main difference, as I saw it, was that in Bulgaria people drink and have fun. In Australia young people drink with the objective to get drunk and therefore throwing up is material evidence and proof of having achieved that objective, hence the feeling of pride.

These subtle waves of culture shock I was experiencing daily, as well as the occasional cultural tsunami, were amusing at times but more often than not, especially in the first few years, a source of great frustration. However, during my university life in Australia, or four or five years into my Australian adventure, my faith in the Australian experience was restored. Furthermore, I started to feel more liberated, ironically because that's when my own stereotypes of Australia and Australians were challenged.

It was then, and especially from my second year of university on, that I could see that the people I had met at school were not necessarily representative of the general Australian population. This meant that there was hope I would meet my kind of people amongst the thousands of students at Western Australia's oldest university. I met a girl who singlehandedly managed to change my freshly formed stereotypes of Australian girls and she is still one of my best friends more than 15 years later. Her name is Louisa Anne Jones, now Kimberley-Bowen, and she was a science student who loved reading European literature, going to the art gallery, and watching foreign films, and she was willing to skip class to go to the movies with me in the middle of the day. Furthermore, she was the best-dressed girl I had met in Australia, not to mention the most decent human being.

My general perception of Australian girls up until then was derived exclusively from my experience at school, a very proper school, where at least in theory I should have been able to meet girls I find interesting. In 2013–2014 it was the single highest ranked Western Australian school in terms of academic achievement. But the girls in my year (back in the late 1990s) fell neatly into three distinct categories.

The first was the type that wear unisex Billabong sports gear, play five different sports a week, do not wear lipstick, do not read foreign literature, or any literature beyond what is required at school, and were not academically oriented. Then we had the type that was studious, conscientious and probably intelligent, who read literature; strictly English literature, of course, but they were too conservative to venture outside of their little group and clung to their group of like-minded girls as though their identity depended on it.

Finally, we had the gang of first generation Australian girls of Greek, Italian and Macedonian parents who were extroverted, and vivacious, but again, like the others, were not interested in history or art galleries.

You can imagine how excited I was to meet Louisa, and in the same year, several other young men and women, particularly her best friend, the refined Michael Auty, who to this day comprise my closest friends here. Over the years I have noticed that my closest friends in Australia are all of the purely Anglo-Saxon variety, but and this is a significant but, they have all lived a part of their life in Europe.

Just as I was settling in at university, a most disturbing incident took place; an incident that plunged me into excessive self-analysis for days. I discovered how my new Australian friends viewed me and exactly which box they had placed me in.

At the age of 20 I was left speechless when I discovered that one of my good friends from university considered me Australian, not Bulgarian. We were sitting on the grass overlooking the Swan River, a few steps away from the main university cafeteria (UWA has one of the most romantic campuses in the world) debating (as is the fashion for young university students, naively thinking ourselves experts on international affairs), when I referred to myself as a Bulgarian.

My friend quickly interrupted and said, 'But you are not Bulgarian. Your parents are. You are Australian!' I will never forget how disturbed I was by that comment. Was it not a huge compliment to be considered one of the locals, so to speak, in a country I had only inhabited for about five years?

After some extensive thought (yes, I was spending a lot more time dissecting my thoughts and feelings than studying) I realised that during those vulnerable years, when I was still planning to return to Bulgaria full time after my undergraduate studies, I felt threatened that I had lost some part of what it is that makes me Bulgarian in my own eyes and in the eyes of those around me. I already felt an acute sense of loss because I had missed the end of high school in Bulgaria, and even at 20, I was much too young to consider the advantages of having lived in two different countries, being fully immersed in another culture. I was still so preoccupied with what I felt I had lost by being away from my home country.

I did not realise it then, but I seem to gravitate toward people who call more than one country home. I have come to the conclusion that if you are someone who calls more than one country home, you will be forever noticing cultural differences on the surface, below the surface, and everywhere else. With time, they simply become less personal and therefore less of a source of annoyance. In fact, they can even be amusing.

Let me share something here purely for fun. I like to go to gallery openings. But gallery-going in Australia was still a qualitatively different experience to gallery-going in Bulgaria, and not because of the art on display. First of all, when you enter a Bulgarian art gallery, you will be confronted by people of all age groups, from retirees to young students in jeans and sneakers. People are not there for the wine and cheese and to be seen, they are there for the art, and if you listen to the conversations around you, you will learn something new about the genre of art on display.

In Australia, you will find a cross-section of society at a gallery but generally speaking the people who truly understand art and appreciate it are not the ones who can afford to spend the thousands of dollars a single painting can cost here. The people who can afford the art in Australia, and who represent a large proportion of the gallery attendees, tend to be the rich housewives (and occasionally wealthy businesswomen or men) with oversized pearls and bold designer handbags, who never fail to make me giggle with their favourite phrase and standard comment on any and all works on display, 'Oh, darling, isn't it exquisite?'

Having made the above statement public I will now have to keep track of my own usage of the words darling and exquisite. I realise that some of my observations stated above may sound like complaining. However, recall what I told you about Bulgarians—our national mode of meditation is complaining. At least this is interesting complaining.

CHAPTER TWELVE

Misunderstandings and little-known facts about socialist Bulgaria

I must confess, you are not the first person who has endured a highly detailed account of my Bulgarian childhood, and I am reasonably confident you won't be the last either. However, even when I feel I could not be any more comprehensive and clear with my accounts and stories, I am often baffled by my friends' questions and wonder exactly what have they grown up hearing about Eastern Europe. I say Eastern Europe instead of Bulgaria, because most people I have met in Australia have no idea how to locate Bulgaria on a map and once they do, they immediately ask if it was a communist country and therefore, to them, automatically Eastern Europe.

It slowly occurred to me that my shock at their questions and their surprise at my answers was largely due to an absence of a common frame of reference. What they thought of as everyday life in a socialist country in the 1980s was not at all my Bulgarian experience. What they imagined when they thought of Eastern European school life, play and entertainment, was not even remotely close to my Bulgaria. They thought there was no play and no entertainment. Fashion, culture, food, the list went on and the gap grew wider.

Consider these little-known facts about life in Bulgaria during our socialist years provided by academic Pavel Pisarev in the international journal *South-East Europe Review* (2006, issue 3) and pay attention to your own reaction. The following is my personal summary of Pisarev's findings or at least the findings that I find most interesting. In socialist Bulgaria:

- 80% of families owned their own home (apartment or house).
- 60% had a second home—a villa in the country (usually inherited from grandparents or other relatives).
- Education was free and compulsory.
- School books were free of charge.
- School lunches were free of charge for students.
- Health care was free and provided through an extensive network of polyclinics, specialised health clinics, general multi-specialty clinics and hospitals.
- Hospital medicine was free.
- 60% of employees and workers were sent on 14-day vacations with their families to either Black Sea resorts or mountain resorts (bear in mind Bulgaria has many health spa establishments).
- Unemployment was practically non-existent.
- High life expectancy, low death rate.
- More than 200 scientific institutes and universities and cultural centres (bear in mind population eight million).
- 50 puppet and drama theatres.
- 20 operas, operettas and symphony orchestras, without counting the scores of museums scattered all over the country.

I have pointed these numbers out to two Australian friends and their reactions were interesting. One simply could not believe it; he had not thought that Bulgaria would have an opera or theatres, let alone many of these, although he could not account for why he thought that. The other said that it was not surprising socialism collapsed and left the country broke, all that free stuff was excessively generous and unsustainable.

Pavel Pisarev correctly points out that none of these would be possible in the absence of economic stability and prosperity in the country, and this is something else not known in Australia, that Bulgaria was a prosperous society for a big part of its socialist days. If you were to spend a little bit of time researching publicly available data, you would find that Bulgaria was (at various stages of its socialist experiment) among Europe's leading countries in its production and export of:

- Memory devices, software and personal computers—Bulgaria was the first European country to mass produce computers, starting with IMCO 1, followed by IMCO 2, which is believed to have been reverse-engineered from Apple II Plus, and then the series of Pravetz computers, Ptavetz-8, 8M, 8A, 8D, 8C, 8S (the most advanced model), and the Pravetz-16 series, which were compatible with IBM and PCs, to name a few. In the last years of communism, Bulgaria was still the number one producer and exporter of computers for USSR, producing 40% of the computers used across the Soviet Union and the Eastern Bloc. For more information, consult the presentation by the former Deputy Minister, Ministry of Economy at World Bank, Julieta Hubenova from 2012, or Bulgarian computers on pravetz.info.

- Output of electric power (energy sector expanded dramatically in the 1960s and this resulted in the appearance of dozens of dams, hydroelectric power plants, as well as the Kozloduy Nuclear power station with its six reactors).

- Arms.

- Zinc.

- Lead.

- Electric trucks (in 1986 Bulgaria's Balkancar was the third largest producer of forklift trucks in the world, after Federal

Republic of Germany, and Japan; the US came in fourth and in 1988 Bulgaria produced one-fifth of the world's electric trucks, and it ranked first in the world in production per capita).

- Tobacco.
- Attar of roses.
- Cheese (you can buy two types of Bulgarian feta cheese even in Australia).
- Grapes.
- Tomatoes (in 1974 Bulgaria was Europe's biggest exporter of tomatoes, beating Italy, with 755,000 tonnes of tomatoes).
- And second in the world in wine exports (after France). In fact, Socialist Bulgaria even exported wine for the UK market and for the USA in 1972.

The point is, and this point is important because a lot of young Bulgarians themselves have no idea that in the years of my childhood Bulgaria had both industry and agriculture. By the end of the 1950s Bulgaria had become an 'industrial-agricultural' country. I quote from Emil Giatzidis' 2002 book, *An Introduction to Post-Communist Bulgaria: Political, Economic and Social Transformations*. 'Many experts agree that Bulgaria's achievements, at least until the 1980s, were spectacular. For example, the economic historian, Derek Aldcroft is quoted by Lampe to effect that Bulgaria "has been one of the great success stories of the 20th century, with the highest rate of economic growth in Europe and a degree of structural change second to none"' (Lampe, 1986; 8).

In the 1960s the communist leadership had placed the emphasis on light industry, agriculture, tourism and information technology. Speaking of IT today, in post-communist times, did you know that the Global IT IQ Report ranks Bulgaria eighth in the world and first in Europe, based on the number of IT professionals—8844 in early 2000s?

Also worth mentioning, and something else not commonly known, is the fact that in Bulgaria, agricultural production increased rapidly following collectivisation, and this is in contrast to other countries in the Eastern Bloc, where collectivisation had a rather negative effect. I cannot fail to mention that, in spite our close relationship with the Soviet Union, who were Bulgaria's biggest trading partner (with some estimates showing more than 60% of Bulgarian exports being swallowed by USSR), we also traded with Western Europe (a fact not commonly known), especially West Germany and Italy.

As you may have guessed, the collapse of the Soviet Union had devastating consequences for Bulgarian exports post-1989, but onto more pleasant information. France's Renault and Italy's Fiat had made deals with Bulgaria to build their cars aimed at the Eastern Bloc market, in factories in Bulgaria. Bulgarrenault made cars based on Renault 8 and 10, and Pirin-Fiat made cars based on Fiat 124 and Fiat 850.

Speaking of cars, for anyone interested in socialist era cars, Google Trabant, Moskvitch, Lada, Skoda, Jigyla. I still fantasise about driving around the country in a freshly painted bright red Trabant.

Logic dictates that a country's economic prosperity will vary from decade to decade, and Bulgaria started showing signs of reduced economic growth by the 1970s, to be witnessed in the late 1980s. Some of the main factors cited in Emil Giatzidis's book as causes of the economic crisis in the late 1980s are 'a downturn in agriculture, slacking of technological advance, pricing anomalies leading to ineffective allocation of resources, diminished competitiveness of exports, decrease in the production of consumer goods' and not to be underestimated, significant financial losses due to financing clients such as Libya and Iraq, who turned out to not be 'prompt payers'.

The collapse of the communist government in 1989 saw a foreign debt of $10 billion, compared to two billion in 1984. I cannot pretend for much longer to be immensely interested in economics and economic planning inefficiencies, but I think a page of discussing exports should be sufficient to arouse your interest so you can continue this education on your own.

Something else that seems to be experiencing a significant decline since my childhood is the state of the Bulgarian military. Do not misunderstand, I am certainly not a fan of anything military oriented (except military parades—the theatrical marching arouses patriotic feelings in me). In 1989, the year communism collapsed, Bulgaria had an army of 108,000, and in 2014 it was 26,000. More precisely, in 2014 our army was roughly 24% what it was in 1989.

I don't know about you but I am wondering exactly what kind of employment these 80,000 plus who are no longer employed by the army happen to enjoy these days—private security company bosses, bodyguards? That would mean they are in heavy competition with all the former boxers and weightlifters no longer trained and sponsored by the state.

In 1989 we had 2200 tanks, in 2014 just 80 (that is less than 4% what it was in 1989). Of heavy artillery systems (whatever that means), we had 1450 in 1989, 96 in 2014 (less than 7% what it used to be), military ships—120 in 1989, six in 2014 (exactly 5% what it used to be), military planes—230 in 1989, 16 in 2014, rockets (Skad and CC-23)—24 and eight respectively in 1989 and in 2004. However, as a condition for entry into NATO all of these were destroyed.

In case you are wondering about Australia, with nearly three times the population of Bulgaria, it aims to expand its army personnel to 31,000 by 2014–2015 (if you include navy and air force, it goes up to 57,000), and it operates 51 military ships and 59 Abrams tanks (according to Australian Defence Force information available on the internet).

Following yet another interesting diversion in my spontaneous discourse, I should return to my original complaint—the lack of information in Australia regarding the greatness of Bulgarian exports in the years of my childhood. I understand that not everyone in Australia, or anywhere else in the world for that matter, will know precisely what Bulgaria produces and exports or how many theatres and opera houses we have, and I am not suggesting that they should, although they would be infinitely cooler if they did.

This reminds me of a question my Australian dentist asked me about Bulgaria and it perfectly illustrates my constant irritation with Australian ignorance about all things Bulgarian. This intelligent, well-travelled man (although not necessarily around Eastern Europe), when told that I was off to Bulgaria and sadly could not book online tickets to the opera in Sofia, confidently asked, 'Oh, does Bulgaria have opera?'

I do not expect Australians to be familiar with Bulgarian opera history or to even know that some of the greatest opera singers in the world are Bulgarian (Boris Christoff, for example, was 20th century's number one bass in the world, Gena Dimitrova, Raina Kabaivanska). It is possible that most of these people may not even know Australian opera history. I am certainly no expert on opera houses around the world. But to know that Bulgaria is one of the oldest countries in Europe and to not assume that it would have an opera house?

I was infuriated, so much so, my anger acted as anaesthetic to such an extent I actually had a semi-pleasant dental experience. I emailed my dentist photos of the eight opera houses in Bulgaria a week later and I noted that there are eight opera houses for a population of just eight million people. I should also mention that my mother was horrified and worried that 1) I have wasted my time, instead of studying, looking up and downloading and emailing photos of opera houses to our dentist and 2) that I had taken an innocent, if ignorant, comment so personally. She therefore concluded, and informed me in no uncertain terms, that she was questioning my emotional stability and general mental health.

I have met a few young Australians who are surprised to hear that Bulgaria produces anything, let alone that we were leaders in the productions of something, and during our socialist years at that. I am sure that many Australians also don't know much about France or Italy's economy, exports, or even culture, but they still show a level of excitement about those countries; they have heard good things, and they have seen romantic images or some famous landmarks of those countries, and they would not even contemplate to question their ranking on a corruption scale. But as soon as you mention an Eastern European country in Australia, grey preconceived images of the Cold War variety pop up involuntarily.

Consider these observations made by the Australian journalist George Negus, who lived in Italy for a year and wrote about it in his memoir *The World from Italy: Football, Food and Politics*. He informs us that it is common knowledge that Italy is 'endemically corrupt, legalised and bureaucratised to the point of stagnation, and utter frustration' where 'it was estimated that something like 60% of all Italian business and political activity was under Mafia influence' and where 'most Italians live in cramped domestic surroundings' where the kitchen, living room, office and laundry are one and the same room. Yet we never talk about any of the above when we discuss our travels to Italy or our plans for visiting Italy. We never begin by saying, 'but Italy is corrupt and they have the Mafia'. Instead, we continue to romanticise Italy only focusing on what's great about the country—their fashion, the food, the architecture. And isn't that lovely? I am in favour of such positivity. How about we extend that attitude to cover Bulgaria too?

Australians I have met over the years have the expectation that, when they ask an Eastern European (and all Eastern Europeans are the same to them) about their country and their life before they moved to Australia, the answer would be a sad story of repression, depression and subdued colours everywhere. That's why they usually don't ask. Since the question is never asked, we each go on believing what we have always known and believed, unquestioned, unchallenged and ultimately misunderstood but without even knowing we are misunderstood.

Being 15 when I moved to Australia, I had no idea what stereotypes Australians held of Eastern Europeans and their countries. I did not even know that there had been an active anti-communist propaganda at Australian universities until I was in my twenties. I bought my father the memoir of a British-born academic, Raymond Priestley, about his years at the University of Melbourne as a Vice-Chancellor, (1935–1938). In this memoir it is briefly mentioned that academics were not allowed to teach Karl Marx's philosophy and anyone suspected of being a communist or teaching communism in any form had to be reported to the authorities.

Because no one, up until my university years, had asked me anything about life in Bulgaria, I had no idea how little Australians knew about Bulgaria. Until, that is, I would venture out and indulged my nostalgia by telling an Australian friend how great Bulgarian life is, the way people relate to each other, the culture, the theatre, the music, the food. You should see the Australian reaction. It starts as a blank face, immediately followed by shock, a deep wrinkling of the foreheads and silence, while looking for a diplomatic response. Then it comes, 'Wasn't it a communist country? You had no freedom of speech' and 'Is it true you couldn't own your own home?'

We already know the answer to the second question—Bulgarians owned their own homes and did not live in communal apartments, sharing a kitchen and a toilet with several other families like some Russians did. But the first one, freedom of speech, seems to be a favourite concern of anyone who considers themselves educated, or dare I say it, an intellectual.

I, as a Bulgarian, have a deep-seated fatalistic streak and do not believe freedom exists, in the way most people think of it. I think it is a grand and lovely illusion, perhaps a necessary illusion but an illusion nonetheless. But I am also optimistic by nature; ironic, I know, and I like Yuri Aikhenvald's interpretation of human freedom, 'Human freedom does not consist in the choice of an action, but first and foremost, in the choice of a reality.' Lucky for you, simply the act of reading this book means that you are familiarising yourself right at this moment with my chosen reality.

But I must, at this ever-so-important juncture, find a heavy and reliable Bulgarian voice to express an opinion on the subject of freedom. The seeds of objectivity must occasionally be allowed to pop up even on this sentimental journey on an imaginary train.

I am instantly reminded of the diary of a famous contemporary Bulgarian writer, Stefan Tsanev, titled *The Devils in Hell Will Clap for Me* (trust a Bulgarian to assume there is more than one devil) which covers his musings and opinions about life and art in the years before the collapse of communism, from 1978 right up to 2002 (12 years in a free market economy).

In his diary, Stefan Tsanev writes that complete freedom (which he does not define) brings out the worst qualities in Bulgarians—'greed, desire for revenge, pettiness, hunger for power'. I should point out that Stefan Tsanev is as anti-communist as you could find, and even he observes that during Bulgaria's time as a socialist country there was 'categorically' good literature, good theatre, good art, 'especially art in opposition'. He writes about foreign European actors and theatre groups visiting Bulgaria and expressing envy at the sheer number of Bulgaria's permanent theatre troupes.

One of our most legendary actors, Tatiana Lolova, who has finally published a memoir, also makes a similar observation. Nedialko Yordanov, another one of our most prominent contemporary poets and playwrights, writes in one of his several memoir volumes, that in its socialist days Bulgaria had 54 permanent theatres across the country, each with its own building, its own set of actors. They were from various cities or towns across the country; all of them guaranteed accommodation and all other necessary resources.

Both Nedialko Yordanov and Stefan Tsanev believe that the purpose of art is to be in opposition to the ruling establishment. In fact, Stefan Tsanev believes that it is impossible for a poet to be on the side of the strong and therefore, no self-respecting poet would be on the side of the ruling elite. Both artists enjoyed periods of time during which their works were unpublished or out of favour with the communist leadership, presumably for being excessively critical of the prevailing socialist elite.

I have a tendency to instinctively trust writers and poets because I perceive them to be not only more observant than others but also more honest and more motivated by noble ideals.

In case my chosen reality about Bulgarian life in the years of my childhood seems a little overly sentimental and peachy, I need to include the opinions of severe critics of the system. As you can see, even the critics share my love for the Bulgarian way of life and the Bulgarian spirit, in spite whatever ideological or other objections they may raise. I suppose I need to familiarise myself more closely with the reasons behind the rejection these authors suffered, perhaps call a former secretary for ideology (yes, they did exist, as a legitimate and paid job).

On a serious note, even Stefan Tsanev writes that, while some writers may have gone unpublished for many years or were even publicly criticised by the communist leader himself, as Nedialko Yordanov was (for a sold-out play, which was perceived to be openly making fun of the ruling elite, in particular the head of state), the way the regime induced writers to write in the prevailing 'socialist realism' fashion was not by sending them to concentration camps (as many Westerners would believe), but by bribing them with 'apartments, cars, medals'.

What many of my Australian friends fail to appreciate is that writers in Bulgaria were put on a pedestal in the years of my childhood, and what they said and wrote mattered, because they were widely read by the general public and therefore of great relevance in influencing public thought and opinion. In a more capitalist society like Australia, prominent and acclaimed writers do not enjoy such wide readership and influence with the general public and therefore their opinions may be expressed as freely as a bird flies, because they are largely irrelevant in the grand scheme of public thought; they exert influence over a small and select part of the general population.

Many of my young Australian friends may find it interesting that even in Australia certain books were forbidden back in the 1960s and no, not only the communist manifesto. One of my closest Australian friends, Kirsty Hine, has recently presented me with a book by Ramona Koval, *By the Book: A Reader's Guide to Life*. In this book the author talks about all the books she has read throughout her life, and how each of these books has shaped each period of her life. What a romantic idea that is, to document the books that mean so much to you and why. The reason I mention this book here is because it was Ramona Koval who informed me that in Australia in the 1950s, '60s and even the early 1970s, books that are considered classics were banned in Australia. The titles may shock you—James Joyce's *Ulysses*, DH Lawrence's *Lady Chatterley's Lover* (banned until 1965), and Henry Miller's *Tropic of Cancer* (banned until 1973).

Speaking of freedom, and often this construct is associated with another broad concept: democracy, I am reminded of Jonathan Dimbleby's book, *Russia*, based on his travels across the vastness that is Russia. Having read this 542-page study, as a Bulgarian I could relate to some of what the Russians he met told him. I also found myself at times disagreeing with his interpretations of Russia, but the book is clearly written by a distinguished author (as the back cover states) and is well-researched, considering the grand scope of this undertaking by a foreigner.

What really stood out for me, out of 542 pages, was his discussion with a group of well-off St Petersburg 'musicians, artists, academics, designers and writers' on the subject of democracy in post-Soviet Russia. Dimbleby finds himself unable to comprehend or relate to responses such as, 'But, my friend, don't speak to me of democracy. I don't believe the word has any meaning in the modern world.' Or 'Why democracy? Is Germany free? Or America? Democracy for Russia would be death because people don't like democracy at all,' or 'Democracy is not right for Russia. We don't need it. We need strength.' He finds their attitude to democracy irresponsible, I find it fatalistic and realistic.

Something else Dimbleby found incomprehensible is that Russians do not seem to associate democracy with personal freedom. The very same people, who told him that they don't believe in Western-style democracy for Russia also told him that they feel they have freedom, 'But I am free, I can say what I like to you.' Or 'We have dictatorship already, so we are free.'

This also reminds me of something Shirley MacLaine shared in one of her memoirs about the cultural differences and the differences in thought between her and a lover of hers, a famous Russian director. She pointed out that she simply could not understand him when he told her that Russians need a dictator; no other form of leadership or government would suit his people.

George Negus wrote about the Italian's perspective on freedom in *The World from Italy*, and here's what he had to say, 'To them freedom is fragile and imperfect. It's relative. It has never been and never will be absolute. It's an ideal, a principle, a goal, an objective, a mechanism—not a tangible thing, and definitely not a system.'

It has just occurred to me that I am referencing Russians rather frequently, but before you are tempted to label me a Russophile I must point out, in my defence, that when you look at the available literature, there seems to be a lot more study and comparison between the Anglo-Saxon world versus Russia than say, Bulgaria. Therefore, I have no choice. Also, Russia has given me Dostoyevsky, Tolstoy, Chekhov, Gogol, Pushkin, Tchaikovsky, Shalyapin, Nijinsky and Chagall.

I will lighten up my monologue with a story that I believe Australians would find of personal relevance and therefore interesting, namely the misconceptions of Eastern Europeans about life in Australia. This shall be a Ukrainian story, not Russian. In the early days of life in Australia, as a teenager, I was mostly interested in forming friendships with other Eastern Europeans because I felt they would understand me better, and naturally, I was delighted to meet a Ukrainian girl at school.

After sharing opinions on the books we were reading (I still remember that I was reading a book on Marie Antoinette, she was reading a book on Napoleon's Josephine), we decided to meet at a park. That's where I met this girl's mother, a Ukrainian engineer, roughly my mother's age; early forties.

Now, my 15-year-old self had high expectations for a conversation full of similar experiences and opinions on life in Australia. I was therefore unprepared for the Ukrainian mother's overall evaluation of life in Perth. She promptly informed me that she herself was shocked to discover how poor Australia is and furthermore, she found herself disappointed with life in Perth, which to her was just a 'large village'. At first I thought she meant the differences in cultural life—Perth was not known for its opera, ballet or art galleries—but as it turned out, it was not a cultural poverty she had in mind.

Sure, I was 15 and my expectations were also ignorant and ridiculous, expecting as I was, crocodiles and snakes and needing a helicopter to go to a restaurant, but I never imagined Australia as a poor country, whatever poor means. The full explanation, which clarified her view, was that they expected to find everyone in Australia 'driving a BMW and wearing Chanel' and so far they had seen none.

I must confess, I have lived such a sheltered, protected life, my inner world was so focused on my thoughts and feelings and reading books about other people's thoughts and feelings, that I had not even considered BMWs or Chanel as a benchmark of wealth or even as a measure of any relevance when comparing countries. Most surprising of all was the realisation that Australia was considered poor by a Ukrainian family whose life situation at the time had forced them to sell their one-bedroom apartment in order to pay for their tickets to Australia, after they had lost their engineering jobs and were facing long-term unemployment in a country undergoing a significant and difficult economic and social transformation.

To this day I have no idea what these people had seen or read in Kiev about Australia that led them to form such expectations, but over the years, I have met a number of Eastern Europeans who had previously not had the opportunity to travel extensively, and they too seemed to have unrealistic expectations, which led to initial disappointment with life in Australia.

This may surprise you, but a similar observation and confession is made by a prominent Croatian novelist and non-fiction writer, Slavenka Drakulic, in her book *Cafe Europa: Life after Communism*, which was written in the early 1990s when she was 45 years old. She writes, 'Like other Eastern Europeans, I naively imagined that living in the West automatically guaranteed you a certain standard of living and that such agonising decisions were unknown. The idea that I could be poor living in the West, perhaps unemployed; the fact that there is hardship and financial insecurity everywhere in the world was beyond my imagination.'

What is even more important to note here is that unlike the Ukrainian engineer who had probably not travelled outside of the USSR, the Croatian writer herself acknowledges on several occasions throughout her book the high standard of living in Croatia, the visa-free travel to the West, the holidays in Greece and Spain, the dress shopping in Milan. Yet she too, in spite years of travel in the West as well as Eastern Europe, still lived with preconceived ideas. This should probably be a reminder to us all that visiting a foreign country as a tourist or for shopping purposes will not necessarily give you a greater insight into a culture and a people.

Many Eastern Europeans seemed to think that prosperous societies, such as Australia, would provide all the perks of socialism—free education, free healthcare, extensive network of cultural institutions, ballet, opera, art, theatre, but on top of all that everyone would also enjoy the life of a successful capitalist—island five-star holidays, BMWs and designer clothing. Here we have the first main discrepancy in our understanding and definition of what constitutes 'poor'; they thought they were poor because they had no access to designer clothes or a BMW.

On the other hand, many Eastern Europeans considered the perks provided to them by their respective socialist governments, such as free healthcare, free education, easy access to medical specialists, cheap books, ballet, opera, etc, not so much a socialist model reflecting socialist values, but rather a common sign of a basic civilised society, and as such, these were taken for granted. It was assumed that any decent prosperous society would provide those to its citizens.

I have heard stories of Bulgarians, upon being shown images of homeless Americans living under bridges, concluding that this was nothing more than their communist leadership's anti-American propaganda, because they could not believe that there would be any kind of poverty, let alone homelessness in the world's wealthiest country. In fact, there is a saying I have heard a number of time in recent years from Eastern Europeans, and that is that 'the difference between the East and the West is that in the West, all the anti-communist propaganda is always believed, whereas in the East, the anti-capitalist propaganda is never believed.'

From my personal experience with young people in Australia, it is inconceivable to many of them to even entertain the possibility that their own government may be employing some kind of propaganda. It is almost as if they think that the West has a certain geographic immunity against anything undemocratic or totalitarian. Where I come from, we tend to view everything as some form of propaganda.

This reminds me of something I read in Vladimir Bukovsky's book, *To Choose Freedom*. Bukovsky argued that in the USSR 'we are far better informed about the West than the West is informed about us'. He spent more than a decade in Soviet concentration camps and psychiatric hospitals, and following an international campaign to free him, Brezhnev decided to release him in exchange for a prominent Chilean communist held in a Chilean concentration camp. You can imagine his views on personal freedom would take on a greater meaning than, say, young Russians living in a post-communist country. This is some of what he had to say in his book and bear in mind this book was published in 1987 when Russia was still The Soviet Union.

He wrote that in the USSR 'We know we are constantly being deceived, so we are on the lookout for the lie everywhere. In the West, however, the public is not used to expecting deceptions, so it does not automatically search for it, and thus accepts information in a far less critical manner.'

Finally, and perhaps most interestingly to Westerners, and I am sure Jonathan Dimbleby would be interested too, Bukovsky's opinion on personal freedom, following his escape from the USSR: 'In the fairly harsh condition in which I spent 34 years of my life, I was as free as I am now'. He acknowledged that there was, of course, censorship and even prison, but he argued that everyone had the freedom to choose 'security'. Furthermore Bukovsky explained that censorship created 'a more subtle writing style and a sharpening of the reader's eye'.

Putting aside differences of opinion on life's more abstract themes, such as freedom and democracy, I worry about the stereotypes that have persisted, in spite of the fact that Eastern Europeans have had close contact with or have even lived side by side with West Europeans for some years now. I think part of the problem is that Eastern Europeans, I have noticed, speak differently amongst themselves than they do to their Western or foreign friends and colleagues. This is often a source of great irritation to me, mostly because it widens the gap that already exists in understanding (or rather lack of understanding) between the two and turns it into a black gaping hole full of painful misunderstandings that lead to polite distrust (yes, believe me, it does exist) and consequently a safe distance/coolness we like to attribute to cultural differences.

I have noticed that when Eastern Europeans speak to their Anglo-Saxon or Australian friends about their country they speak in clichés, not knowing where to begin, just how much to say or when to finish, all in the name of being polite. Consider this quote by Mikhail Jvanetsky and ask yourself have you ever sat at a dinner table with an Eastern European and heard them say this? In the early 1990s, soon after the Soviet Union stopped existing Mikhail Jvanetsky wrote:

'Under dictatorship everyone is scared of the question and under democracy—of the answer. Under dictatorship there is more ballet and humour, under democracy—more travel and robberies. As to the large-scale animal fear—just as much in both cases. Under dictatorship you can be knocked out from the top, under democracy—from the bottom. So while our freedom does differ from dictatorship, the difference is not so stark as to be clear to a little-educated person, such as, say, a writer or a military officer.'

I have never sat at a dinner table, or any table for that matter, and heard Eastern Europeans tell their Anglo-Saxon or Australian friends musings like that. I have read such musings in books but never witnessed an actual exchange in person. This monologue excites me on many levels, because as a Bulgarian (born and raised) who lives the bigger part of the year in Australia, I have had the opportunity to hear and read a number of accounts and/or opinions of both Anglo-Saxon and Eastern European individuals regarding life in Eastern Europe now and then. Now and then, of course, stand for the present-day democracies (or whatever you wish to call it) in Eastern Europe and the communist era respectively. And I can tell you that a lot of Anglo-Saxons I know do not know that under dictatorship there is a lot more ballet, let alone more humour.

The Bulgarian professor Peter Emil Mitev writes: 'It was a communist regime alright, but how does one explain the fact that the world congresses of sociologists and philosophers and the annual UNESCO conferences were held in Bulgaria?' How indeed? I can tell you that a lot of Anglo-Saxons I have met would be shocked to hear that last sentence; western style democracy and soviet dictatorship not that different.

Now I have family friends and have indeed welcomed an Anglo-Saxon into my Bulgarian family, I can personally confirm the level of surprise the British express at the Bulgarian health care system. The strength of the Bulgarian health care system lies in the strong traditions in diagnosing correctly. This is true even today, when funding is often insufficient and now quite expensive, particularly for those who need it most—pensioners. They are amazed at 1) how quickly you can see a specialist, 2) how thorough the testing is, including ordering expensive scans and 3) most importantly, the correct diagnosis and subsequent treatment of a condition they had spent years in the UK being treated for without a proper diagnosis and without much improvement.

Maybe the problem lies deeper than I originally thought. There must be more to it than the way Eastern Europeans talk to their Western European friends. There must be more to it than what Eastern Europeans choose to share with their Western counterparts. Maybe we really are so different we are destined to be at least partially misunderstood and confused.

I came to this realisation when I read Slavenka Drakulic's *Cafe Europa*. I read her book and I was confused. Sure, there are several obvious reasons that may be used to partially explain my inability to relate to her story as completely as I had hoped. For starters, she is of a different nationality; I am Bulgarian, she is Croatian. We have the age and generational difference, given that she is approximately 30 years older than me. Also, her book was written in the 1990s, when she was 45 and it should be interesting to see what she thinks of Eastern Europe in the 2010s, when she is in her late sixties.

But allow me to dissect my own confusion, which may also show exactly how confused, say, an Australian reader may be upon reading her account. At first I was excited that finally I could read, in print in the English language, certain truths about the standard of living under communism. She was refreshingly honest when she explained that the standard of living was high, that there was free health care, nice clothes and that as a Yugoslavian (although she insists on referring to herself as a Croat) they also enjoyed greater freedom than many other Eastern European countries, particularly in the form of visa-free travel to the West. She points out that Yugoslavs used to travel abroad precisely for the purpose of shopping and mentions going shopping for a dress in Milan, and holidays in Spain and Greece. She also mentions a holiday home, a nice car. Sharing that information alone would help Westerners slowly change their perceptions of Eastern Europeans as donkey riders waving a communist manifesto. In fact, life so far seems better than normal, even rather cosmopolitan, what with the international travel.

But in spite all this, and this is the confusing part, she is still dissatisfied and in the extreme. Immediately following these examples of the standard of living, she writes that, 'Yes, essentially it is a comparison between prison cells.' What is confusing is that there is never a mention of her work as a writer being censored or threatened in any way. There are no examples of family being persecuted in any way. Her biggest issue appears to be that during communist time she became sick of the constant 'us' and 'we' in public speaking, and her inability to start with an 'I', her dislike of parades, other sweaty comrades, the mud which seems to appear all over Eastern Europe when it rains, and her biggest issue—the suspicion and cross examinations she had to endure as an Eastern European travelling abroad (even though her Swede husband also endures the Croatian suspicion toward Westerners).

She writes about all Eastern Europeans as 'us' yet she is often quick to mark herself as different, as a Croat, as somehow not one of us. I realised that at times she sounds like someone who wishes to differentiate herself from other fellow Croats too. But for someone who seems confident in expressing herself, she is not quite clear on what it is she really wants from her state, what it is that would have comprised her ideal society, beyond that 'the important thing is that we finally learn not to take orders.' Yet there are no clear-cut examples of her taking orders. Her complaints seem abstract in the absence of personal examples of persecution.

Perhaps most confusing for me, and disappointing, was the lack of discussion about Croatia's cultural life during communism; no mention of literature, theatre, opera, book publishing, and she herself is a writer. I kept reading and kept recognising truths on many pages of this book, but the overall feeling the book aroused in me was that of the ever unhappy, dissatisfied, victimised Eastern European, and this after she had already told the reader how well off Croatians were during those years.

Could it also be that we as a bunch tend to be reflective and analytical of the world around us and therefore will always find something in this great big scary world to make us feel a little sad? Could it be that as a writer and an artist she has the propensity to simply always be in some kind of opposition?

I could not shake this unpleasant yet familiar voice. But how could I describe that voice? It's a voice I have heard before. It is the voice of some Eastern Europeans I myself have encountered. I think I can at least attempt to give it a name—it's the voice of low self-esteem, not personal or individual self-esteem, but national identity self-esteem, and how our mother, the motherland, has not given us as much as other mothers (foreign countries) have given their children.

This is how Westerners become confused about this mysterious and 'suspicious' part of Europe—Eastern Europe; because their knowledge of Eastern Europe, outside of propaganda in their own country, is often derived from Eastern Europeans who suffer from low national identity self-esteem. Is it part of the Eastern European personality, to be critical of the motherland, of the system, of fellow countrymen?

Look at a country like Sweden (coincidently, this is where Slavenka Drakulic spends a lot of her time these days). I met a few Swedish and Norwegian students who were completing exchange studies at my university in Australia, and the impression I got, from casual conversations about life in their home countries is that the standard of living is high, they enjoy a lot of perks education-wise that can only be described as socialist in nature, they are not afraid of the word socialism but also classify their countries as 'civilised'.

During a group discussion in a management class, a Norwegian student explained that in Norway CEOs would receive a salary 1/10th of that received in the USA, yet, he himself cannot imagine many people choosing to leave Norway. There was no talk of dissatisfaction, no comparisons of what you could not get in Norway that could be obtained in other countries, no complaining in general could be detected.

A few years ago the popular talk show host, Oprah Winfrey, travelled around the world and compared how people outside of the USA lived. The segment I remember best is the segment on Denmark. She interviewed two professional, well-paid women. One was an architect and they were both full of praise for their country and their lifestyle. No, they did not mind the 65% tax rate, because they 'could see where that money was going'. No, they did not mind that they lived in tiny two bedroom apartments with kitchens the size of a box, and where the architect lady had all three of her children share a bedroom so small Oprah extended her arms and they almost reached both walls. They liked the society they live in, the fact that people care about others, not only themselves, that they could choose their professions and that there was not much of a difference in the level of pay between different professions.

Is that to say that life across Sweden is really that idyllic and perfect? Not if you read Eva Gabrielsson's memoir, partner of the late Stieg Larsson, author of The Millennium Trilogy (*Girl with the Dragon Tattoo* series). She writes: 'It's strange that Sweden always seems like a model to many other nations, when here we have the same problems found everywhere else.'

She also describes that in the 1990s 'New taxes, a staggering rise in interest rates, a drop in construction subsidies … The real estate sector took a huge hit, with many firms closing or resorting to massive layoffs. When I lost my job as an architect, Stieg and I entered a period of very tough times.'

Not to mention that as a journalist, he was working to expose Sweden's neo-Nazis and there were grave fears for his safety. She goes on to say, 'In the 1990s more than a dozen people were murdered in Sweden for political reasons by individuals involved with neo-Nazi groups.' Journalists were the victims of car bombs, and in 1998 there were more than 2000 'unprovoked racist attacks'.

But not even the Trilogy has given Sweden the label of a country where sinister things can happen and Swedes themselves do not seem to be readily basing their national identity self-esteem on events or periods of national hardship or crisis. Some years ago I remember Denmark was listed as a country with one of the highest rates of youth suicide in the world, but you will not find a shortage of Danish nationals telling you everything that is great about their society. They tackle their problems in the absence of complaining and sweeping generalisations. We should think about that, particularly we, the Eastern Europeans.

These days I find myself somewhat less sensitive about the overall level of ignorance I encounter when it comes to my Bulgaria, be it from Westerners or a select few Bulgarians. Perhaps it's because I am older, at 37 now, and presumably more emotionally stable. Maybe it is because I have been too busy for a few years now, with something fulfilling—inducting my husband and my three mini-me sons (a third son arrived in the course of writing this account) into the sacredness that is Bulgaria, and reliving my Bulgarian childhood through them with every annual stay at home. Or maybe it's reading other Australian's accounts of their own travels and encounters with ignorance, this time by Europeans about all things Australian.

I recently read a book romantically titled *Left Bank Waltz* by Elaine Lewis, an Australian middle-aged lady who opened an Australian bookshop in Paris, on the Left Bank of all places, in 1995. She talks about her French doctor's reaction upon hearing her decision to return to Australia to have surgery, and quotes him as saying, 'I don't think anyone in Melbourne will be able to do that kind of micro-surgery.' Or Robert Dessaix, who was asked by a Frenchman if there was any culture in Australia.

Now that I mention it, I recall a dinner in New York where a young American woman asked my husband, 'Australia? Isn't that a country of convicts?' and then wanted to know if kangaroos just hop about on the streets. So yes, you could say I feel a little better knowing that there are negative stereotypes floating around the sacred aura of fabulous countries like Australia.

Oh no, it just occurred to me that what I have really admitted to here is that I feel better in the knowledge that ignorance is everywhere, not just when it comes to my Bulgaria. Alright, no need to overanalyse; it simply means I am not perfect. I am flawed and that is consistent with what I stated earlier, namely, that Bulgarians do not much care for perfection.

CHAPTER THIRTEEN

The many layers of homesickness

As a 15-year-old teenager I missed the obvious about Bulgaria—the family, my friends and the food. Up until the age of 17 to 18 my homesickness could be explained exclusively in terms of missing the physical proximity and face-to-face contact with my grandparents, my cousins and my friends.

I also missed my great-grandmother's cooking and typical Bulgarian foods such as Bulgarian feta cheese, lutenitsa (tomato, roasted eggplant and pepper dip), *lukanka* (magical Bulgarian dry sausage), *kiopulo* (roasted eggplant dip), the famous Bulgarian natural yogurt, and the sweet Bulgarian tomatoes, especially in a *shopska* salad (tomatoes, cucumbers, onion, peppers all drowned in sunflower oil, topped with grated feta cheese and a pinch of salt). I should point out that there are no tomatoes on this planet sweeter than a Bulgarian tomato. Even Jean-Claude Van Damme will tell you that; he came, he filmed a movie and fell in love with our sweet tomatoes. The last sentence should be interpreted literally.

After a few years and by the time I reached 19 or 20 years of age, I started to miss the country itself. I missed the smells of Bulgarian forests and the mountains, the smells of the Burgas Sea Gardens overlooking the Black Sea, the statues in the parks, the public parks, and even the smell of cigarettes in cafés, in spite of the fact I do not smoke.

By my early twenties, I had found a better balance between life in Australia and life in Bulgaria. But again, because a much bigger part of the year was spent in Australia, I found myself feeling a deeper longing—I missed the sense of constancy, stability and permanence I experienced during my childhood in Bulgaria, and which I clearly still associated with Bulgaria. More precisely, what I was really missing was my childhood. By this stage of my life homesickness had become multi-layered; I was now missing the family and friends, the food, the country and my childhood.

At that particular time, in the mid-1990s, given the political and economic situation in Bulgaria, there was no clear, objective reason to feel or to expect that life in Bulgaria would bring me greater stability than life in Australia; quite the opposite, in fact. Clearly, this layer of homesickness, the nostalgia for my childhood, may be better explained by the fact that I was in my twenties. A woman's twenties are not a time of great inner stability; you are beginning adulthood, yet you are still in training (many years of university study ahead of me), unable to exercise full control over your life, still unaware that you never reach the stage of life where you have complete control of your life and so you dream of the idyllic, simpler times when your world was much smaller and predictable.

A journal entry from this time reads: 'I experience such joy when I see my great-grandmother sitting in her usual corner of the couch, asking the same questions, having the same worries. Maybe that's why I actually like it when, even today, she still comes into my room in the middle of the night to check if my blanket is still covering me, because if it isn't 'the child will catch a cold'. I can stay home and watch her all day, because to me she symbolises unconditional love, stability, permanence. This city symbolises stability. This home, this country, symbolise permanence and stability.'

By my late twenties, I was better able to verbalise my love for Bulgaria. A journal entry from 2007 (age 28) reads: 'I am reading the book *Born to Rule* by Julia Gelardi about five of Queen Victoria's granddaughters, who became Queens of Europe. I have just read an entry of Queen Marie of Romania and I find that her words about England describe my love for Bulgaria best: "Something deep within me responds to England as it does to nothing else. To the soil, the people … warm pride budding up from my depths when I think of England … something deeper than reason, something fundamental, so to say basic.'" For me, it's a biological connection, above and beyond verbalisation; it's a profound physiological reaction every time I step on Bulgarian soil.

During my twenties, as I was getting a stronger hold on who I really am (again, only people in their early twenties are this preoccupied with 'finding themselves'), I felt that Bulgaria was an integral and most central part of who I am. I felt that just about anything my Australian friends thought of as uniquely Regina could really be explained almost exclusively with the fact that I am Bulgarian. To this day, it still shocks me to discover the obvious, that there are in fact Bulgarians out there who are quite different from me.

This probably also accounts for my obsession with Russian literature. I felt that the Russian soul was much more similar to the Bulgarian psyche than the Anglo-Saxon, and I read and re-read all 19th century Russian classics available in Australia— *Anna Karenina*, *The Idiot*, *Notes from Underground*, *Crime and Punishment*, *The Brothers Karamazov*, Chekov's plays, all of which were a life-changing experience. People who do not believe that books can change your life should read 19th-century Russian classics or Bulgarian classics, but sadly, these are harder to find.

My journal shows my perception of the Russian mentality at the age of 22, 'I find that Russian people are soul-searchers who attribute an enormous amount of significance to every single emotion they happen to experience. It's as if they live in the name of intense emotion, yet they still maintain a certain hope, sentimentality, and romance.'

I continued to read every biography out there, from Chagall, Nijinsky, Shalyapin and Catherine the Great to biographies of Lenin and Stalin and even the recent travel memoirs of Sofka Zinovieff (*The Red Princess*) and Masha Gessen's *Two Babushkas*. Reading these books helped me remain close to home when so far away, in spite the fact that these women's experiences were vastly different from my own. Somehow their manner of expressing their feelings and talking about their life felt familiar and close to me.

It was perhaps inevitable that the conversation would once again focus on books but this is important because I have an interesting fact to reveal here about myself, and yes, it does have something to do with my book interests. You see, before I developed an obsession with Russian classics at 18, I was obsessed with Oscar Wilde's writing, first *The Picture of Dorian Gray*, when I was 17 and then his plays. This very Bulgarian girl was obsessed with the English wit, or at least the wit of Oscar Wilde's characters, which is so different from Bulgarian wit.

'It is absurd to divide people into good and bad. People are either charming or tedious.' 'All women become like their mothers. That's their tragedy. No man does, and that is his.' 'If I am occasionally over-dressed, I make up for it by being always immensely over-educated.' 'The whole theory of modern education is radically unsound. Fortunately in England, at any rate, education produces no effect whatsoever.' 'Now produce your explanation and pray make it improbable' 'The good ended happily, and the bad unhappily. That is what fiction means.'

I was even writing about Oscar Wilde in my diary, 'If this diary shows slight contradictions, it is only the result of my wisdom. Oscar Wilde said that, "the well-bred contradict other people. The wise contradict themselves." After all, only the shallow know themselves. So far, following Oscar Wilde's logic I am wise. I do also preoccupy myself with ideas of what is right and wrong, and according to Oscar Wilde this is a sign of "arrested intellectual development". So even Oscar Wilde contradicts himself; he must be wise.'

After Oscar Wilde, I was also interested in French literature; again anything European that might bring me in touch with my Bulgarian spirit. I did not find much similarity between the French psyche and the Bulgarian soul. My early-twenties self felt that 'French people need to view themselves and have others view them as a little mysterious.'

My experiences with the French mentality were based exclusively on my opinions of Balzac and Guy De Maupassant's characters. Subsequently, I have read just about every published travel memoir about Australians who have moved to France, and you will be surprised just how many of these books are out there.

Eventually, I had to also face what was right in front of me, the Anglo-Saxon psyche. My impressions of the Anglo-Saxon soul were based exclusively on my opinions of the kids I had gone to school with in Perth, rather than on characters from English classics. My journal reads: 'They strike me as the kind of people who need to know the rules and obey the rules in order to be happy.' Now bear in mind, I was in my early twenties when I made such observations, a time of personal development best characterised by the excessive use of sweeping generalisations. Some of these generalisations make me cringe but they also amuse me greatly and even make me laugh today.

The front page introduction to my 1999 journal entry (21 years old) reads: 'What you are about to participate in is a biased and subjective account of a highly dynamic life story, which as it branches out, develops a tendency to spit out the tiny seeds of objectivity. There will be no overwhelming spills of objectivity; just here and there, to give flavour to the original story. And just like a tree, the story will expand, branch out, make connections at 100 km/h, develop new neural pathways, and yet may still be stuck in the middle of nowhere.' You have to laugh when you read such over-confident, self-absorbed nonsense.

You are probably thinking how ironic it is that my closest friends in Perth are of the Anglo-Saxon variety, and wondering, with all that Bulgarian pride and patriotism, couldn't I find a few Bulgarians in Australia? The irony is that the small number of Bulgarians I have met here (with few exceptions) are people I found myself distrusting and disinterested in because I found them to be petty and envious. This was most unexpected even for me, given my natural propensity to romanticise all things Bulgarian and I needed to resolve this discrepancy in my mind.

I am happy to report that I have found a solution to this obstacle that stands in the way of romanticising all things Bulgarian. More precisely, I have chosen to believe that envious Bulgarians comprise a small percentage of the overall Bulgarian populations; so small, in fact, as to be called outliers. Anyone who has studied statistics at university will tell you the best thing to do with outliers is to delete them from your data set and exclude them from further statistical analysis. I certainly do not want a few Bulgar outliers to ruin the nice conversation we are having on this imaginary train.

In my mid-twenties an extra layer of homesickness emerged rather forcefully—I started to miss not only Bulgaria the country, my family and friends, and the food, but the Bulgarian lifestyle and the people. Most of all, I missed the Bulgarian conversations with all the complaining, the jokes, the brutal honesty and the genuine exchange of feelings.

I missed the loud exchanges on the street, on the trams (there is no place more quiet than a Perth bus), the café culture where people sit and sip on the same cup of coffee for two hours, not because of the coffee, but because they are so engaged in an intimate conversation. But we do have great coffee in Bulgaria too.

I am not the only one who places such importance on conversations. In his first memoir, the Australian Robert Dessaix writes about his time studying in the Soviet Union, 'I liked the nights spent talking about important things, about ideas, around kitchen tables. Russians know how to converse in a way we don't.' He goes on to say, 'It's a time for self-revelation, gossip, passion, argument, negotiation, mockery, sometimes even cruelty. I loved it. It was uncompetitive. There were never just two sides.'

Years later, in his latest memoir, Dessaix has dedicated an entire chapter to conversation and thanks to him, I have developed a fondness (such an English word) for a couple of 18th century Englishmen, Henry Fielding and Samuel Johnson, purely based on their thoughts on the importance of conversation. Henry Fielding said, 'The grand business of our lives, the foundation of everything, either useful or pleasant, is conversation.' and Samuel Johnson said, 'There is in this world, no real delight (excepting those of sensuality) but the exchange of ideas in conversation.'

When I speak of missing the Bulgarian lifestyle, I really missed my city walks, and the walks in general. In Perth, people take walks but they usually drive to a river or a nice lake and walk around it. In all these years living here I have never been asked by an Australian friend to go for a walk in the city centre. The city centre is built exclusively as a business district for the purpose of working and as a place for shopping; you go to the city to work or to shop, or to have a business lunch, but not to take casual walks and catch up with friends.

I like meeting friends who work in the centre and walking to a nice restaurant, I do dates with my husband too, since he is right in the centre and conveniently close to our house, and it feels nice but the atmosphere has a more corporate feel than a lunch in the centre of Sofia.

Now that I think about it, a lot of things in Australia are purpose built and designed. If you want to walk, there is a park for you, Kings Park; a magnificent park with all sorts of rare plants and trees and the largest of its kind in the world, located right next to the centre of a city (according to guides on Perth river cruises). The view from Kings Park of the river and city skyline is incredible; Perth has the prettiest skyscrapers in Australia, but that is all you can do in Kings Park, walk and enjoy nature and the view.

If you want to shop, you need to get in a car and drive to one of many giant shopping malls with 200 shops under the same roof, but you cannot do anything other than shop there. There is no view to enjoy and no other signs of civilisation. Life is ordered and structured and simplified, but it can at times read like a business plan, and business plans generally lack romance and spontaneity.

That is why I love our suburb in Perth—it is different from most other suburbs in that, while it has character—an Australian character with its federation style houses—it offers a European lifestyle. Dutch TV has labelled it 'ritzy' in a show on Perth but I don't think that is the right word, it has romance and allows for spontaneity; it is comprised of many little specialised shops, bakeries, a lot of different cafés and restaurants, bookshops, small health clinics, hospitals, schools, markets, parks. All of these are located right in the centre of suburbia, within a few minutes (walking minutes, that is) of your house.

Best of all, with two of our boys now attending school, we have become close friends with several other couples whose children go to the same school. Since we are also neighbours we now engage in spontaneous activities that remind me of my life in Bulgaria, down to the crayon drawing on the street, bike riding around the suburb, weekend get-togethers and even camping and holidaying together.

These days my husband and I get on our bikes and ride down the road to meet our friends and get a drink or dinner at one of our local bars or restaurants. Truth be told, we often drive but Fiona and Matt Davis, Rebecca and Chook Easterbrook, Claire Lemonis and Regina and Paul Oakeley always ride (or run, or yoga down the road, as Australians do).

This is not common for an Australian suburb; a typical Australian suburb is comprised almost exclusively of houses, sometimes near-identical-style houses, and if you want to go for a walk, there is nothing to see but other houses. If you want to go to the shops, you need to get in a car and drive some distance to the closest shop or shopping centre. If you want to go to a café, again, you need to fill up that car because you will have a nice drive to locate the nearest one.

If you want to catch up with people, again, you will need to book it in a week in advance. That applies even to the most exclusive suburbs, with the difference there that you are looking at beautiful mansions rather than houses, and you might have a nice view of the ocean or the river, but again, any other human needs beyond having a roof over your head need to be indulged after you have gotten into a car and driven some distance.

This is something else that requires getting used to in Perth— an almost exclusive dependence on a car. A car here is almost as important as your legs. I find that a touch depressing but now that I am a mother of three boys, I spend a lot of time driving and I am determined to enjoy it. I take the kids for drives around all the romantic parts of the city, around our suburb, around the river, lovely trees lining our way, the sun shining above us even in winter. With nice music in the background, they fall asleep, and I call it meditating. It easily classifies as the most relaxing time of my day in Perth. This is an experience I can only enjoy in Australia. I cannot do that in Bulgaria.

In Bulgaria driving and relaxing will never be spoken in the same sentence. A relaxing drive does not even exist as a phrase in the Bulgarian language (OK, I exaggerate a little). Perth, on the other hand, is built for driving; the streets are wide, no one is beeping, the car spots are large, there are always places you can go to and enjoy the view from your car. In Bulgaria, the streets are narrow, not always particularly even, there are many other cars and people coming at you from all directions, at lightning speed, beeping, yelling; there is nowhere to park and you can never enjoy a view from the car.

In my mid-thirties, I find myself slightly more grounded and stable, probably because with three kids and a husband, life has become more about others and less about me. But let's not get too carried away. If I am unable to make it back to Bulgaria for a month every year (and this has happened a number of times due to study or pregnancies) I still feel like not everything is right with my world; I do not feel as settled or grounded.

Having said that, I now also find myself quite at home in Australia. Maybe it's because of my husband, Carrick, who as his name suggests is not remotely Bulgarian, yet is the only male human being with whom I can ever imagine myself sharing a life. My romantic self would also like to point out an interesting fact to which I attribute a great deal of romantic significance—Carrick and I were married on the same date, 7th January, that I arrived in Australia for the very first time as a 14 year old (just three months short of 15) exactly 14 years later (purely by chance, that is when the venue we liked was available).

Maybe Australia has started to feel like home because I have been able to find a Bulgarian-like routine in our suburb, where I can walk from my house to my favourite bookshops, and minutes after buying a magnificent book or 10, I can pop into a favourite café or walk to the shops, bump into people, rather than cars, all the while witnessing other signs of civilisation.

With three small children I don't really get to enjoy the cafés much, but sometimes just seeing others enjoying themselves in a café while I am buying nappies is enough. These days, when the kids go to sleep, I can leave them with the husband and go bike riding around the suburb with my next-door neighbour. Yes, even in Australia it turns out you can be close to your neighbours.

In this case, she is not exactly purely Australian; she is a German countess, who still spends time at the family castle in Germany. Yes, it is ironic that I would be a friend to a countess, given that I have already made fun of aristocrats on this very train. I assure you, she does not mind. After all, she is a countess who likes to raise rats (all right, guinea pigs but to me they are just cleaner rats or pig-rats as I call them). She is completing a PhD in biology so I forgive her. We indulge in something else that is very Bulgarian, namely complaining, even arguing politics, sharing intimate family gossip, usually hers, as I am very boring in this department.

Another surprising fact—it turns out that bikes do not have to be ugly and helmets do not have to make you look like an alien. A couple of years ago my husband presented me with a most romantic-looking bike for Christmas. It is bright red with a gorgeous basket in front, and it comes with a fabulous white retro helmet, more like a motorbike helmet, only more sophisticated (and the custom-made bell Louisa bought me to go with it). Most importantly, it turns out you can ride a bike and really firm your behind without bringing on a sweat; you will recall my feelings about sweating.

As I have gotten older, and ironically after seven years of minimal sleep due to three babies who never sleep, my outlook on life between Australia and Bulgaria has become significantly more settled and serene. I ride a red bike with a basket, for goodness' sake!

Having gone through many layers of homesickness, I have finally reached the stage of appreciation for my Bulgarian-Australian lifestyle. It no longer has to be one or the other, it can quite happily be both, a Bulgarian and an Australian life, depending on the time of year. The great privilege of dividing time between two countries, however unevenly it may be at this stage, is that life becomes rich and dynamic in ways that cannot be described with words or experienced in one country alone. These statements may sound obvious and perhaps even cliché, yet it has taken me more than a decade to begin to experience my life in those terms and to see it in this light.

Most enjoyable of all, for me, is that even though I lead a life in two very different countries, I have still managed to live in more or less a bubble of my own choosing. That is to say, I am able to enjoy what is best about both Australia and Bulgaria while largely ignoring all changes or aspects of life in these countries that displease me.

When I am in Australia I still miss Bulgaria, the Bulgarian lifestyle, my family and friends, my homes, even my books there, but I am there often enough and importantly, for just long enough to enjoy only the best of what Bulgaria has to offer and avoid all else that may displease me.

Ignoring what displeases me and choosing my own reality is something I have had to do, in light of my particular life experiences. Alright, that last statement sounds a little melodramatic but all joking aside consider the central issue of my early years—asserting my independence from my parents and observe what life has thrown my way. Just as my teenage-self was desperate to free herself from parental control, I was sent to Australia, the other end of the world, for three years with only my parents. Then after years of struggle for liberation, I am accepted at the very same university where not only one but both of my academic parents work (although fortunately in different departments).

Finally, as a young adult, having chosen a husband, married and bought a house, I still find myself not only in the same suburb but down the road from my parents. They can drive home and still check if my lights are on. So you see, the universe is laughing in my face and I have had to surrender to some extent, relax, learn to mediate, and ultimately ignore what displeases me.

By focusing on mostly what pleases me I have chosen my preferred reality. Of course, now that I have made claims of mastering my reality, I have probably jinxed myself. I will have to light some candles, look for some holy water and cross my fingers. I am Bulgarian, I am ever-so-slightly superstitious, and I am joking; I have never had possession of holy water of any kind and lighting candles in a house makes me nervous I will cause a house fire.

After all that boasting about finally achieving balance and harmony between my Australian and my Bulgarian life, I must also confess a most undesirable occurrence, some of which you are experiencing right at this very moment, simply by having to listen to me on this imaginary train. You see, as I started to miss Bulgaria with all its natural beauty and the Bulgarian people and their lifestyle, I also found myself becoming intensely patriotic. You could say a patriotic wave swallowed me up and spat me out, raving superlatives about all things Bulgarian. As my patriotism surfaced, I also seemed to develop a strong concern for the perceptions of foreigners, such as yourself, of Bulgaria.

I am now facing another dilemma, because I find that just like the famous Russian dissident, Vladimir Bukovsky, people ask me questions about Bulgaria that are 'impossible to answer briefly, and no one would listen to an answer in depth'. But I am starting to feel optimistic now, because I feel that you and I are changing this right at this moment. After all, you are sitting next to me on a moving train, unable to escape, and therefore, although you may not be willing to listen to an in-depth answer, you have little choice right now.

Robert Dessaix argues that a conversation, as opposed to idle chitchat, is 'an exchange of ideas, insight, information, and feelings that change the participants'. Therefore, I have no choice but to conclude that our conversation on this train is no idle chitchat. I fully intend to change you or at least, whatever preconceived ideas you may have about Bulgaria.

But, and here lies the problem, Dessaix explains that conversation has to be 'polite, it has to please your companions, refrain from violent outbursts, or anything that might bore, stifle or anger anyone present'. Unfortunately, that is too English for me, and you will recall I am Bulgarian, and as such, I cannot in all honesty make such grand promises, such as never to anger my companions. But I can promise to always express my true feelings and insights.

CHAPTER FOURTEEN

A taste of Bulgarian food greatness

The moment I pour olive oil or sunflower oil into a pan and the second the onion starts cooking and begins to release its smell, I think of my grandmother and my great-grandmother. I think of our talks in the kitchen, I can see us sitting around the table in the dining room.

From there, an entire network of memories rush back to possess my entire being. Memories about Bulgarian summers and Bulgarian winters, Bulgarian jokes shared around the table and Bulgarian music, spontaneous dances around the table.

Then I think about more food—the smell of tomatoes, basil, parsley, mint, Bulgarian herb *chybritsa*, ripe peaches, apricots, cherries, watermelon, snacking on capsicum stuffed with feta cheese and Bulgaria's magical sausage—*lykanka*, or *diado* and the world's best dip—*lutenitsa* on bread. If my cousin and I were particularly good we would get a Bulgarian favourite dessert—*mliako s oriz* (milk with rice and cinnamon) or baklava.

I don't know a single Bulgarian living abroad who does not miss Bulgarian food. The sheer diversity of the Bulgarian cuisine is a big surprise to foreigners. Every single year for the last decade my husband has expressed shock at the size of the menus not only in Bulgarian restaurants but even in the most low-key cafés, which will offer a menu of about 20 pages, full of at least ten different salads, numerous entrees, hot and cold soups. The mains, lo and behold—stews, casserole, duck, rabbit, pheasant, vegetarian, fish, pork, lamb, veal, and not just a single signature dish but entire sections of various dishes including all of these different types of meat and fowl.

The richness of the Bulgarian cuisine is due to a diverse geography and a warm climate, which provide the right conditions for a large variety of vegetables, herbs and fruits to grow. That and a rich tradition in cooking based on more than 1330 years of Bulgarian history (add a few thousand more years if you include the influence of the other great ancient civilisations on Bulgarian land before us).

I have a number of Bulgarian cookbooks but they are all in Bulgarian and I am yet to come across a Bulgarian cookbook in English in a bookstore in Australia. However, having googled Bulgarian cuisine, a book did come up, which seems to be highly recommended by a few Anglo-Saxon names and it is *The Bulgarian Cookbook* by Ivailo Piskov. It comes in paperback and as an e-book and contains 143 recipes. Another book, which looks impressive, is *Traditional Bulgarian Cooking* by Atanas Slavov, also offering around 140 recipes.

A great website, which offers a nice introduction to Bulgarian cuisine with a few recipes is www.findbgfood.com/bgmeals.htm. But I would like to offer a few of my favourites to cook right here, adapted for Australian cooking. Naturally, the same dishes will taste better in Bulgaria (and when cooked by a more experienced cook).

In Australia, in the absence of ceramic pots and hot plates, I find stir-fry woks to be a great substitute. My husband bought and carried a large ceramic pot in his hand luggage, as well as a heavy hot plate, but fear of breaking them (I am Bulgarian; I keep special things for special occasions) has meant I don't often use them and rely on a nice red wok.

Before I relay some of my favourites, which I can cook (there are plenty of favourites I still can't cook) I should mention that as diverse and rich as the Bulgarian cuisine is, most main dishes are cooked following the same principle—on low heat, and always with a great variety of fresh, local vegetables and a number of herbs and spices, olive oil or sunflower oil and onion. This not only makes the Bulgarian traditional meal very delicious and rich, but also extremely healthy.

All meals start with a traditional Bulgarian salad, accompanied by a shot of *rakia*, one of Bulgaria's national drinks, and as you may have guessed, strong spirits. It kills all the bacteria in your stomach, as my grandfather would say, as it is usually 40% alcohol and it can be made from plums, grapes, peaches or apricot. My grandfather makes his own *rakia* and his own wine at our weekend house; a hobby he has perfected over the years. This is followed by a main meal with or without soup and, of course, wine or beer. Dessert is usually fresh fruit, especially in summer.

However, because of the number of varied ingredients, the taste of any one given dish will vary slightly depending on who has cooked it and exactly in what proportion each ingredient has been added. Bear that in mind when I say that my Monastery Gyuvetch is not necessarily the same dish as another Bulgarian's Monastery Gyuvetch.

Now let us have an exciting time immersing ourselves in some Bulgarian cooking. Please keep in mind that you are being instructed by someone who is a spontaneous cook, who likes to improvise with food; I am more of a passionate cook than a highly precise one.

Chicken and chorizo sausage *sach* (pronounced 'such')

In the absence of a hot plate use a wok.

- 1 kg chicken breast, boneless
- 2 chorizo sausages
- 250 ml chicken stock
- 1 clove garlic, chopped
- 5 tbsp paprika
- 3 tbsp oregano
- salt and pepper
- 1 chilli
- 450 g mushrooms, white mushrooms or portabella if a stronger taste is preferred
- 2 capsicums, sliced
- ½ cup light olive oil
- 2 tbsp butter

Serves 4

Place olive oil in a wok and cook with the chorizo sausage for five minutes on low heat. Then add the chicken breast chopped up in cubes with the paprika, salt, pepper, oregano and garlic and mix well. After mixing it well, add the butter, and cook for five minutes. Then add the sliced capsicum and a small amount of chicken stock and stir well.

After five minutes add the mushrooms, the chilli and more chicken stock, and cook for a further 15 minutes on low heat, while mixing well and adding stock in small quantities every few minutes. Overall cooking time is 30 minutes.

Moussaka

There are a number of different types of moussaka, not to mention the Greek moussaka, but I find the Bulgarian style moussaka to be the most delicious. This is my own version, which I cook in Australia. Also, my favourite Bulgarian herb, called *chybritsa*, cannot be found in Australia and as a substitute I use oregano, but of course, the taste is not quite the same.

- 500 g pork mince
- ½ cup olive oil
- 2 cloves garlic, finely chopped
- 1 onion, finely chopped
- 4 tbsp paprika (sweet Hungarian paprika, or 2 tbsp sweet paprika + 2 tbsp smoked paprika)
- salt and pepper to taste (but I like 1 tbsp of salt)
- 1 tbsp cumin
- 2 tbsp oregano
- fresh parsley
- 6–7 medium-sized boiled potatoes, cut in small cubes
- 1 can tomato puree, or 5 fresh tomatoes pureed
- 1 chilli, chopped (optional)
- 2 spring onions, finely chopped

Serves 4

Boil the potatoes for 20 minutes or until soft, then peel and cut into cubes. While the potatoes are boiling, cook the pork in a wok in olive oil (1/2 cup or enough to cover the entire bottom of the wok) and with the paprika, salt, chilli, oregano and cumin for five minutes on low to medium heat. After five minutes, add the onion and the garlic and cook for 15 minutes on low heat. Then add the tomatoes and cook for another 20 minutes on low heat. Transfer the contents of the wok into a baking dish, spread out the mince mixture from the wok and mix well with the boiled potatoes. Add the finely chopped spring onions and mix into the baking dish. Cook in the oven at 180C for 15 minutes, or until it starts to look golden and baked. Overall cooking time will be 55–60 minutes.

When feeling a little lazy, I add the cubed boiled potatoes with the pork in the wok and keep it all cooking in the wok while mixing well.

Monastery Gyuvetch

- 2 ½ cups Arborio rice
- 1 kg pork, diced chunky
- 500 ml water
- 2 onions, finely chopped
- 450 g mushrooms
- 2 capsicum, sliced
- 1 sliced chilli (optional)
- ½ cup olive oil (I always use the lightest flavoured variety)
- 4 chopped butter
- 5 chopped of paprika (optional—a spoon of smoked paprika)
- 3 chopped oregano, salt and pepper
- a handful of fresh parsley, finely chopped

Serves 4

Place the olive oil, enough to cover the entire bottom of the wok, and heat for a minute with the paprika, oregano, salt and pepper. Add the pork and cook while mixing well with the spices for 10 minutes on low heat. Then add the onions and the capsicum. Cook for two to three minutes, mixing well, then add the rice, mix well and add three or four tablespoons of butter. As the rice cooks, while constantly stirring, add the water and chilli. Once the rice has been cooking for 10 minutes with the other ingredients, add the chopped up mushrooms and cook for another 15–20 minutes on low heat. Add freshly chopped parsley on top. Overall cooking time will be approximately 45 minutes and it serves four.

The same dish may also be cooked with chicken instead of pork.

Steaks in natural yogurt, smoked and melted cheeses

This sounds exciting and to the Australian ear, rather unusual and adventurous, but it is delicious.

- ○ 4 pork loin steaks
- ○ 1 cup Greek-style natural yogurt, in the absence of the famous Bulgarian yogurt
- ○ 1 packet of smoked cheese, 200–300 g
- ○ 1 packet of processed cheese that is wrapped individually, of the 'Laughing Cow' variety
- ○ 1 cup warm water
- ○ ½ cup olive oil
- ○ 3 chopped oregano
- ○ salt and pepper

Usually we would cook this dish in a traditional Bulgarian ceramic pot, but in Australia any roasting dish will do.

Marinate the steaks with salt, pepper, oregano and three tablespoons of olive oil and do it thoroughly and individually. It is important to use a lot of oregano and a lot of pepper to give the steak the right intensity of flavour, so be generous. Ideally, leave the steaks marinating for 15–30 minutes but it is fine to proceed with the cooking immediately if time is an issue. Using a stir fry dish or any pan cook the marinated steaks on low heat for five minutes or so on each side, or until at least half cooked.

Take the baking pot or roasting dish and place ½ cup of olive oil on the bottom of the pot, add the warm water, add the four steaks with their juice from the stir-fry pan, and cover the entire top surface of the steaks with blocks of spreadable cheese and thick sliced pieces of smoked cheese. Once that's done use a spoon to cover everything in sight with natural yogurt, about 1 cup; imagine it as icing on top of a cake. Put the lid on or cover the dish with foil and cook in the oven at 180 C for 1.5 hours. Cook uncovered for the last 20 minutes or so.

Chicken drumsticks in beer and butter

- 6–8 chicken drumsticks
- 7 boiled medium sized potatoes
- 12 tsp butter
- 1 bottle beer (330 ml, any type of beer will do)
- salt and pepper
- 2 chopped oregano
- 1 onion, sliced thickly

Serves 4

This dish could not be any easier to make. Cut seven or so potatoes in half and boil in water for 20–25 minutes until soft, then peel the skin off and cut up into smaller cubes. While the potatoes are cooking, start cooking the chicken. Pour the beer into a roasting dish and place in the chicken drumsticks. Use your fingers to sprinkle the top of each drumstick with oregano, salt and pepper, then place one teaspoon of butter on top of each drumstick. Place the same number of teaspoons of butter around the chicken, to swim in the beer, and cook in the oven for 40–45 min on 180 C. After 45 minutes of cooking, remove the chicken from the oven and place the boiled potatoes, chopped up into cubes, in with the chicken and turn the drumsticks over. Use a spoon to baste the chicken with the beer and butter sauce, just enough to wet it. Then add the thickly sliced onion all around the chicken and potatoes and cook for 20–25 minutes or until the chicken and the potatoes look golden. Overall cooking time for the chicken is one hour and 10 minutes.

Diced pork and onion in tomato sauce
- 5 onions, chopped chunkily
- 1 can tomatoes, or 5 fresh tomatoes pureed
- ½ cup olive oil
- Salt and pepper
- 1 kg diced pork, chunky
- 5 chopped paprika (try sweet Hungarian paprika)

Serves 4, eat with Bulgarian Shopska *salad (see page 175)*

Heat the olive oil in a pan with the paprika, salt and pepper for a minute or so. Then add the pork and cook on low for 25 minutes. Once the meat starts to look lightly coloured, add the onion, chopped up in chunky pieces, and cook for another five minutes before you add the tomatoes. Mix the tomatoes well and cook for another 15–20 minutes on low heat. Overall cooking time will be 45–50 minutes.

Lentil soup
- 1 onion, finely chopped
- 5 tbsp paprika (try sweet Hungarian paprika)
- 3 tbsp oregano
- 3 tbsp tomato paste
- 5 tbsp olive oil
- 2 chicken stock cubes or 1½ L chicken stock
- 2 celery sticks (optional), finely chopped
- 2 tsp sea salt

- o 1 spring onion, finely chopped
- o 2 carrots, chopped chunkily
- o 2 cups whole green lentils
- o 1–2 tbsp butter (optional)

Serves 4

The great thing about this Bulgarian soup is that you can toss all the ingredients in in one go and let it cook itself on low heat for 1.5 hours.

Use a large saucepan and put either three litres of water with two chicken stock cubes OR place 1.5 L chicken stock and 1.5 litres water, add the lentils, onion, garlic, paprika, oregano, oil, tomato paste, salt and butter, and cook on low heat for one hour. After one hour, add the carrots and celery with the spring onion, all chopped up and cook a further 30 minutes, again on low heat; this is important. It may be cooked without the chicken stock; I simply like the flavour. It is usually eaten with some bread on the side (any European variety will do) and some *Shopska* Salad *(see page 175)*, when cucumbers and tomatoes are in season.

Bean soup

- o 2½ cups of red kidney beans, dried
- o 2 garlic cloves, finely chopped
- o 1 onion, finely chopped
- o 4 tbsp paprika (try sweet Hungarian paprika)
- o 3 tbsp oregano
- o 3 tbsp tomato paste
- o ¾ cup olive oil first cold pressed, light flavour
- o 2 tbsp sea salt
- o 1 spring onion, finely chopped
- o 2 carrots, chopped chunkily
- o 1½ L chicken stock, or 2 chicken stock cubes

- ○ 2 tbsp butter
- ○ A few leaves of fresh mint finely chopped

Serves 4

This is almost the same as the lentil soup, only you swap lentils for red kidney beans and ideally soak the beans in water overnight before cooking and drain off the water the beans have been soaking in. Put three litres of water with two chicken stock cubes in a large soup pot or 1.5 litres chicken stock and 1.5 litres water. Add the beans, onion, garlic, paprika, oregano, olive oil, tomato paste and salt and mix well by stirring for a few minutes, then cook on low heat for 1.5 hours. After 1.5 hours, add the carrots, spring onion, butter and mint, all chopped up and cook a further 35–40 minutes, again on low heat; this is important. Note that beans take longer to cook than lentils. Overall cooking time will be just over two hours. Bulgarian soups are generally eaten with bread on the side, and, as you would know by now, *Shopska* salad *(see page 175)*.

Tarator

This is my favourite cold soup, and just about every Bulgarian will eat this throughout summer as an entrée. I personally like it thicker and saltier, with more garlic, but depending on taste you should experiment with the amount of salt, garlic and olive oil you put in.

- ○ 500 g natural yogurt (in Australia I buy the Greek style natural yogurt, but Bulgarian yogurt is most suitable for this)
- ○ 1 large cucumber, peeled and cut into small cubes
- ○ 3 garlic cloves, crushed (if you like less garlic stick to 2 cloves)
- ○ 2 tbsp olive oil
- ○ freshly cut dill, finely chopped
- ○ ½ tsp salt

- ○ 2 cups of cold water (if you prefer it thicker; 3 cups if you like it lighter)

Serves 2

In a large salad-sized bowl add the yogurt, crushed garlic, salt, olive oil, and the cucumber and mix well. Then add the water slowly and take your time, mixing well. Sprinkle the dill on top.

Airian–cold yogurt drink

I love this during the day. Fill up a glass with water halfway, then add three tablespoons of natural Greek yogurt, a few drops of olive oil (optional), a pinch of sea salt and mix well for a minute or so. I have Australian friends who love it and make it themselves.

Green salad

- ○ 3 spring onions, finely chopped
- ○ 10 romaine lettuce leaves (red leaf lettuce is also fine), cut into thin strips
- ○ 10 radishes, chopped in quarters
- ○ 6 tbsp light olive oil,
- ○ 2 tbsp vinegar (apple cider vinegar)
- ○ 1 large cucumber, sliced chunkily
- ○ 1 tsp salt, or less if not a salty person

Note: the olive oil and vinegar must be mixed in well with the salad. You will know you have mixed it well when you notice a fine layer of olive oil shine on each of your lettuce leaves. Cut up the cucumber, lettuce, radish and spring onion, add the salt, olive oil and vinegar and mix well for a good minute. Only use the light flavoured olive oil.

Shopska salad

Even here there are variations, and in Australia, for simplicity, I use tomatoes, onion, cucumber, olive oil, salt and a pinch of vinegar (optional) but no peppers.

- 5 medium tomatoes, chopped chunkily
- ¾ of a medium-sized cucumber or ½ of a large cucumber, chopped chunkily
- ¼ of a medium-sized red or white onion, sliced chunkily
- 4 tbsp olive oil, extra light
- 1 tsp salt, less if you do not like it salty
- handful of Bulgarian feta cheese, sprinkled on top

Serves 2

Important note: Once you have added all the chopped up ingredients in a salad bowl, make sure you spend some time mixing in the olive oil, so that every slice of tomato and every slice of cucumber shines, as it is covered by a fine layer of oil. Then grate some Bulgarian feta cheese on top.

Note: in Australia you can often find Bulgarian feta cheese and Bulgarian goat feta cheese; I am not a fan of goat cheese so I always use the other variety.

Kyopolou

This is a type of dip I love eating at lunch or dinner, or as an afternoon snack on nice bread. It is basically an eggplant, capsicum and garlic dip. Make sure you only use olive oil that has light flavour or sunflower oil. As with most food, Bulgarians tend to make industrial quantities for household consumption, but I will be more conservative with my serving quantities.

- 3 medium-sized eggplants
- 5 red capsicums

- 4 large tomatoes
- 5 garlic cloves but if garlic is an issue use 3 or 4
- red wine vinegar
- 1 cup olive oil
- salt
- small bunch of fresh parsley

The eggplants, capsicum and tomatoes need to be roasted whole in the oven or on a barbeque until their skin is soft and ready to peel.

Once roasted, peel off the skin and put in a Thermomix or food processor along with the garlic, oil, salt and vinegar in order to chop up finely and to mix all ingredients into a dip-type consistency. Transfer to a serving bowl and place the chopped up parsley on top, and spread on nice bread. Once you have tried it you will be craving it for weeks.

Lutenitsa

- 1 kg red capsicum
- 6–7 tomatoes
- 1 large eggplant
- 1 cup light flavoured olive oil
- ¼ cup sugar; I use brown
- 1 tbsp salt
- fresh mint, chopped (optional)

Roast the red capsicum and the eggplant on low heat on a barbeque until the skin is soft and ready to peel. When cool enough to handle, peel the skin off the eggplant and the capsicum and puree together in a Thermomix or food processor.

Puree the tomatoes separately and leave them unpeeled (note: the tomatoes are fresh, not roasted). Transfer to a large pot and add the olive oil, salt and sugar (and mint if you like it). Bring the tomatoes to a boil, then put the heat on low and cook for 15 minutes, stirring occasionally.

Add the eggplant and pepper puree to the tomato mixture and cook, while stirring, on low heat for 15 minutes. Cool off the dip for 10–15 minutes and then store the mixture in glass jars, ideally in the fridge. A word of warning—once you try *lutenitsa* you will need to have it every day of the week. If you find you do not like it, it can only mean one thing—you did not make it correctly. Go to Bulgaria and see how it's done.

Red capsicum stuffed with fresh feta cheese

A favourite afternoon snack for kids and adults alike is this fresh and ridiculously healthy Bulgarian invention. All you have to do is cut a red pepper (or red capsicum) along its side in order to be able to stuff it full of creamy Bulgarian feta cheese. Use your fingers to fill the inside of the pepper and make sure it is a delicious Bulgarian feta cheese you use, rather than other foreign variations. Not only will it fill you up, but it is full of goodness.

There are several other main dishes that are traditional Bulgarian but I leave those to my grandmother, my mother and my aunt to cook to perfection. You must try Bulgarian *sarmi*—stuffed sour cabbage leaves with minced meat, rice and herbs. The Bulgarian pastry *banitsa*, and the Bulgarian wheat-based drink *boza* or *buza*. OK, this one is not purely Bulgarian but it is unique—it tastes simultaneously sweet and sour.

I am satisfied the above instructions are a good introduction to Bulgarian Cooking in an Australian Setting 101.

CHAPTER FIFTEEN

What Bulgaria has given the world

- **The World's oldest golden treasure—
  Varna Necropolis Treasure**

We are not talking about just one golden treasure, we are talking about a country of treasures, scattered all over Bulgaria. The French magazine *Science and Life*, in its 100th issue, names the 100 most significant treasures from medieval times and it ranks the top 25 countries in the world in this respect. Bulgaria is number one, with nine of the world's most important and oldest golden treasures from ancient times.

Bulgaria is home to the world's oldest golden treasure, the Varna Necropolis treasure, which is over 6000 years old (4500–4200 BC) and consists of 3000 items, overall 6.5 kg of 24 carat gold weapons, jewellery and coins. A quick note here to put this in perspective—the Egyptian pyramids of Giza are some 2000 years younger (2589–2504 BC) than the Varna Necropolis treasure.

- **Proto-Bulgarian calendar—The oldest
  and the most exact in the world**

In 1976 UNESCO declared the proto-Bulgarian or the ancient Bulgarian sun calendar to be the world's most accurate calendar, as well as the world's oldest calendar, dating back to 5505 BC. While the popular Chinese calendar dates back to only 9–10th century, according to the proto-Bulgarian calendar, we are currently in the year 7523, rather than 2015.

The ancient Bulgarian calendar follows a 12-year cycle, with 52 weeks (seven days per week), 365 days, (where the first day of the year was the first day of winter and the shortest day) and four seasons of three months each (12 months), where the last month of each season has 31 days, and the remaining two months have 30 days. Every fourth year has one additional day or the 'Day of the Sun'. This calendar calculates the year based on the movements of the sun and Jupiter, and it is based on the solar year, unlike the Chinese calendar, which is based on the moon.

The Bulgarian calendar was circular in shape with 12 constellations, named after the following animals—mouse, ox, snow leopard (*felis uncia*), rabbit, dragon, snake, horse, ram, monkey, rooster, dog and boar. Putting aside the fact that ancient Bulgarians were great mathematicians, the most surprising fact is that in spite its recognised position as the world's most accurate calendar, the Bulgarian calendar was never adopted in Europe.

◦ **Cyrillic alphabet**

Bulgaria gave the world the Cyrillic alphabet. As early as the ninth century AD (850s), the Saints Cyril and Methodius devised the Glagolitic alphabet by decree of the Bulgarian Tsar Boris I, of the First Bulgarian Kingdom, and later, at the beginning of the 10th century AD, the Glagolitic alphabet was superseded by what is now known as the Cyrillic alphabet, developed by students of Cyril and Methodius at the famous Bulgarian Preslav Literary School.

The Cyrillic alphabet is the third official alphabet of the European Union and one of the most widely used writing systems in the world. It is used not only across Eastern Europe, the Balkans and Russia but also across Northern Eurasia (by more than 250 million people, half of them Russian).

○ **The first computer—John Atanasoff**

The first electronic digital computer, the Atanasoff-Berry computer, was invented by the Bulgarian physicist and inventor John Atanasoff (1903–1995) in the 1930s, (1937–1939) at Iowa State University (with Atanasoff's student, Berry, as an assistant).

In 1990 Atanasoff was awarded the highest scientific honour in the United States, the National Medal of Technology. In his speech before presenting him with the award, President George Bush Sr noted that, although Professor Atanasoff had spent his life in the United States, he had always emphasised his Bulgarian heritage and had always been extremely proud of it.

Bulgaria, for its part, has awarded him a number of its own highest honours, and there are, to this day, numerous scholarships and schools named in his honour.

○ **First electronic watch, first wireless heart monitor—Petar Petrov**

Born in 1919 in a village called Brestovitsa, the son of a priest, Petar Petrov became a military officer and part of the Bulgarian Tsar Boris' guard in the 1940s before beginning his studies in engineering. He held degrees in four different disciplines of engineering, spoke seven languages, and following his emigration to Canada and later America, became one of the most prolific inventors of the second half of the 20th century, as well as a NASA scientist.

In 1968 he developed the first ever wireless heart monitor, still used in hospitals around the world, and in 1970 he developed the world's first digital watch, which was given the name Pulsar (named after pulsar stars that emit a beam of electromagnetic radiation). He also developed the world's first computerised pollution monitoring system. He passed away in 2003.

○ **The discovery of the sixth heart tone**

Professor Ivan Mitev (1924–2006) was a Bulgarian paediatrician and cardiologist who discovered the sixth heart tone, also known as the Tone of Mitev. He made the discovery while examining sick children and confessed that the road to this discovery was 'very long, difficult and complicated', but it is still considered one of the greatest Bulgarian medical discoveries even today.

○ **The medicine for childhood paralysis**

Professor Dimitar Paskov is a Bulgarian chemist responsible for some 20 inventions, but his greatest contribution is the development of the Bulgarian medicine, Nivalin, in 1956, for the treatment of childhood paralysis. He is also responsible for the development of a herb-based drug called Belabulgara, which he had patented in the US and which, in 1940 in New York at the 13th Doctor's Congress, was recognised as the single most effective medicine for the treatment of Alzheimer's disease.

○ **Bulgarian contribution to the landing on the moon**

The Bulgarian Ivan Notchev designed the engines for the lunar module *Eagle* used by Neil Armstrong and Buzz Aldrin in the first moon landing.

○ **The inventor Asen Yordanov**

Asen Yordanov (1896–1967) was a Bulgarian inventor, engineer and aviator, who founded aeronautical engineering in Bulgaria. His worldwide fame is due to his prominent contribution to the development of aviation in America, where he holds legendary status. He was considered an authority on all areas of aviation, not only in the theoretical field of plane design and through his famous instruction manuals for military aircraft, planes and submarines, but also for his abilities as a stunt pilot, test pilot and his skill in flying under extreme weather conditions. Neil Armstrong has stated that he, like all American pilots, learnt about aviation from Yordanov's manuals.

Although he passed away in America, and not Bulgaria, a short biography of Yordanov informs us that a sign in front of his house in America reads, 'Asen Yordanov—Bulgarian aviator'. Ah, Bulgarian pride.

∘ Orpheus

In ancient times, Orpheus was known as the greatest singer and musician. There are many legends of his extraordinary powers (from the ability to tame wild animals with his voice to the ability to follow his deceased wife in the afterlife) that his very existence has been questioned by some.

Mythical figure or man, ancient writers tell us that Orpheus was a Thracian born in what is now the Bulgarian Rhodope Mountains, sometime before the Trojan War.

There is, however, a dispute as to where Orpheus' resting place may be, with the Greeks claiming his remains can be found in either Pieria on mainland Greece or Dion, at the foot of Mount Olympus. But I am sticking with the Bulgarian version, proposed by Bulgarian archaeologists and historians—Orpheus' remains can be found in the Bulgarian village of Tatul in Bulgaria's only pyramid, which is older than the Egyptian pyramids.

Historians and famous archaeologists like Professor Ovcharov and Professor Venedikov have presented compelling circumstantial evidence in favour of this theory and this unique and ancient site is known as the Grave of Orpheus and may be visited by tourists. If they are all wrong, the Bulgarian pyramid could only have been built for a Thracian king, and a Thracian king is good enough for me. I will be visiting either way.

∘ Spartacus—The unbeaten gladiator

Spartacus was a Thracian born in 109 BC on what is Bulgarian land today, in a region along the river Struma. Some historical accounts claim he was an aristocrat, others describe him as a soldier who was captured, enslaved and sold as a gladiator by the Romans around 86–85 BC.

After gaining prominence as the unbeaten gladiator in 73 BC, he united 78 other gladiators and became their leader in a planned escape. In a short period of time, Spartacus managed to recruit a small army of followers. Rome promptly sent militia under the command of a Gaius Glaber, but Spartacus, defeated and killed most, and he also defeated a second expedition sent by Rome.

By this time, his army had grown substantially, reaching 70,000, according to some historical sources. Others claim it to have been closer to 100,000 at its peak. It was evident he had had military experience, in order to have been able to manage an army and strategise to conquer Sothern Italy and Roman armies.

It is not clear whether Spartacus simply wanted to free slaves and lead them out of the borders of the Roman Empire or if he was fighting Rome itself, and perhaps that's one reason for the split in his army across various parts of the empire. The Senate was alarmed and sent all their might after Spartacus, and he is presumed to have died in battle. However, the most interesting fact is that his body was never found amongst the 60,000 dead, and his legend continues to grow. In the West his legend has grown, however inaccurately, through movies such as the 1960 Kirk Douglas/Stanley Kubrick *Spartacus*.

○ The Bacillus bulgaricus bacteria

The healing properties of Bulgarian natural yogurt have been known all over the world for some time. One could find Bulgarian yogurt in Holland, Germany, Switzerland and even Japan as early as the 1970s.

The reason for these healing properties (it is believed that regular intake of this yogurt can even extend a person's lifespan) was identified by the Bulgarian researcher Dr Stamen Grigorov (1878–1945), who discovered the Bacillus bulgaricus bacteria. More precisely, he managed to isolate the main bacteria found in natural Bulgarian yogurt in 1905 and his findings were published in the French academic journal *Review Medical*. The bacteria was named Bacillus bulgaricus in honour of his country (it was later renamed Lactobacillus delbrueckii bulgaricus).

Speaking of his country, the doctor was so patriotic that he rejected the most prestigious academic offers in Switzerland and Brazil because he wanted to return to work in Bulgaria. He died in Bulgaria in 1945.

But that is not all. In 1906 Dr Grigorov discovered the penicillin fungi and his findings based on trials of his vaccine with rabbits with tuberculosis were published in the French journal *Le Press Medical*. Unfortunately, at the same time, findings regarding trials of another famous tuberculosis vaccine were already being published. However, the Bulgarian doctor managed to save hundreds of soldiers during World War I when he discovered that soldiers who had been eating mouldy bread did not contract cholera because the mouldy bread they had ingested contained the penicillin fungi he had previously discovered.

○ Professor Krastio Krastev—The Krastev Effect

In 1932, Bulgarian Professor Krastio Krastev (sometimes spelled Krusty or Krastyo Krastev) discovered and began studying an interesting phenomenon, namely that, following an explosion, electromagnetic waves are produced. Furthermore, these waves travel at the speed of light. He named this phenomenon The Electromagnetic Pulse and continued his research in this field, which was considered top secret up until 1962, by which time he had already began working alongside other prominent physicists, among them Einstein.

As a result of this discovery which is now known as The Krastev Effect, it is possible to record each nuclear test in the atmosphere, wherever it may be performed around the world. Because of this, the US and the then Soviet Union agreed on a moratorium on nuclear testing and this consequently tamed the nuclear arms race.

Because of the nature of his work, not to mention that his name is not readily spelled in English, you will have to search long and hard to read up on this professor, but I am here to point out to you the most interesting part of the story—how patriotic the professor was. Even though his work took him to America in 1950, and he died there in 1969, his closest relatives followed his request to have his ashes flown back to Bulgaria because he always wanted Bulgaria to be his final destination. Yet another example of Bulgarian pride. No matter where they go, or how far they travel, Bulgarians always wish to return home.

○ **The world's first female fighter pilot**

The Bulgarian Raina Kassabova became the world's first female fighter pilot, or rather, the first girl, as she was only 15 years old when she flew a combat flight during the Balkan Wars in 1912.

But that is not all, ladies and gentlemen, because Bulgaria can also boast of Maria Atanasova, who was the only female pilot in the world to land a heavy airliner in extreme conditions at London's Heathrow airport, where the *Reading Eagle*'s Wednesday 29th September, 1965 issue, under the heading *Woman Pilots Bulgarian Liner* reports control engineers 'did a double take' when they saw the 'pretty' pilot landing the 'giant' aircraft.

Then there was Emilia Garbova, who was the first female pilot of a military jet, and Valentina Tzvetkova, who is even today, the only female commander of a governmental 'Falcon' in the world. And this, ladies and gentlemen is what I come from (insert wink here).

○ **Sent a man into space (and food to go with him)**

Bulgaria was the sixth country in the world to send a man into space, in 1979, and his name is Georgi Ivanov. Furthermore, and thanks to the work of Bulgarian academic, Tsvetan Tsvetkov, whose team works on developing biotechnology cold preservation, Bulgaria became the third country (after the US and the Soviet Union) to send food into space.

○ **The first solar refrigerator**

The Bulgarian inventor and scientist, Professor Dimitar Chernev (sometimes spelled Tchernev) is a pioneer in the field of solar energy for heating and cooling. In 1980 he invented the world's first solar refrigerator, which has no mechanical or electrical components.

◦ **The farthest planet from the earth**

In 2002 the Bulgarian Professor of Astronomy, Dimitar Sasselov, discovered the most distant planet in the Milky Way, known as OGLE-TR-56b.

UNESCO World Heritage Sites in Bulgaria

Bulgaria is also known for its nine UNESCO World Heritage sites (there are another 14 on the tentative list), which I am certain you are planning to visit in your lifetime. They are:

◦ **Medieval Rock Relief—The Madara Horseman (near the village of Madara, Northeastern Bulgaria)**

This is an early eighth-century medieval rock relief, which is not only a unique work of art but also the only one of its kind in Europe. What is most extraordinary about it is that it is 23 metres above ground level of a 100-metre cliff, which is almost completely vertical.

◦ **The Boyana Church**

This is a 10th-century church in the capital of Bulgaria, Sofia, most famous for its frescoes from 1259, which are great examples of medieval Bulgarian art.

◦ **Rock-hewn churches of Ivanovo**

This is a complex of Monolithic churches and monasteries hewn out of solid rock near the city of Ruse, in the village Ivanovo, best known for the well-preserved 13–14th century Bulgarian frescoes.

◦ **The ancient Black Sea city of Nessebar**

Situated on the southern coastline of the Black Sea, Nessebar is one of Europe's oldest towns. It was colonised by the ancient Greeks in the eighth to sixth century BC and its history is shaped by Thracian, Byzantine, Roman, Ottoman and Bulgarian rule. There are still approximately 40 ancient churches, either partially or completely preserved, dating back from fifth century AD to 14th century AD.

◦ **Rila Monastery**

This is a 10th-century monastery set in the Rila Mountains, south of Sofia (we talked about them in chapter 7). The Rila Monastery is particularly important for Bulgarians because it is considered the cultural and spiritual centre of our national consciousness. It was a hideout for revolutionaries during foreign rule and is the site of a literary school. It is also famous for its Rafail Cross, which shows more than 100 biblical scenes, and 650 miniature figures, all carved with needles, and for its countless murals by Zahari Zograf.

◦ **The Thracian Tomb of Kazanlak**

Located near the town of Kazanluk, in central Bulgaria, this Thracian tomb dates back to the end of the fourth century BC. The tomb is famous for its murals, which are considered to be the best preserved Bulgarian masterpieces from the Hellenistic period. The murals show the Thracian ruler and his wife, a regal feast, their four-horse chariot and various gifts.

◦ **The Thracian Tomb of Sveshtari**

Dating back to the third century BC, in the village of Sveshtari, this tomb is the burial site of one of the most prominent Thracian tsars and his wife. Although the tomb was plundered as early as antiquity, many items are still preserved, such as the ornamental decorations, relief images of women, or caryatids supporting the ceiling of the tomb with two hands, a mural and even the stone beds for the ruler and his wife.

◦ **The Pirin National Park**

Located in the Pirin Mountains, it houses lakes, 1300 species of plant, 160 species of bird, six species of fish, 2090 species and subspecies of invertrebrata and 45 terrestrial mammals. The symbol of Pirin is the flower edelweiss.

○ **The Srebarna Nature Reserve**

This is both a nature reserve and a lake near the Danube River, in the village of Srebarna, in Southern Dobrudja. It houses 39 mammal, 21 reptile, 10 fish, and 179 bird species, as well as 139 species of plant, 11 of which are endangered.

You may have already observed, and if you have not I will explicitly state it for you here, that I have politely waited until the end of this story to tell you what Bulgaria has given the world. Given our entire exchange on this imaginary train, it should not come as a surprise that some form of gloating would eventually take place and now that you have learnt a few things about Bulgaria and what Bulgaria has given the world you must feel I am fully justified in my manner of bragging.

And here we are, at the end of our sentimental journey on this imaginary train of reminiscences and musings. It has been a few hours of spontaneous discourse I have enjoyed immensely, particularly because you have shown yourself to be a most agreeable companion, since you have been unable to disagree or object to any of my claims and musings.

Importantly for me, I have no doubt that even if you are unaware of it, at this very moment, you have been ever-so-slightly Bulgarianised, and that pleases me to infinity and back. I feel that my job here is done. And who knows? Maybe we will meet again one day on another train, be it imaginary or real.

APPENDIX

Resources and fun homework

Art

- Google 'Vladimir Dimitrov—The Master'—3.05 min clip.
- YouTube 'Rilski Manastir' to view some of the icon paintings of Zahari Zograf, Bulgaria's most prominent 19th-century painter.
- YouTube 'Panagyurishte treasure' to see a 6.25 min clip about my favourite ancient Thracian treasure.
- YouTube 'FlyCam Bulgaria St Alexander Nevsky Cathedral Sofia 2014' for a quick and fun aerial shot of this magnificent cathedral.
- Just for fun type 'images of famous Bulgarian paintings' and a nice little selection comes up immediately.
- **http://sghg.bg**—Sofia City Art Gallery.
- nationalartgallerybg.org—Bulgarian National Art Gallery.
- YouTube 'TateShots: Christo' (also look for Christo's Valley Curtain, documentary by David and Albert Maysles) for a quick taste of Christo's environmental art around the world.
- On Facebook check Lyubomir Kolarov, Bulgarian Art and Zhanna Ilieva Art.

Music

YouTube the following:

Opera
- Boris Christoff—*Don Carlo.*
- Boris Christoff—*Le Prophete.*

- Boris Christoff—*Boris Godunov*.
- Boris Christoff—*Mnogaya Leta* (Bortnyansky).
- Raina Kabaivanska—'Ave Maria' (Verdi).
- Raina Kabaivanska and Pavarotti—*Tosca*.
- Ghena Dimitrova—*Turandot*.

Rock, Pop, Metal
- Vasil Naidenov—'*Adaptacia*'.
- Vasil Naidenov—'*Moia Lubov*'.
- Atlas—'*Kukla*'.
- Shtyrtsite—'*Kletva*'.
- Shtyrtsite—'*Sreshta*'.
- Shtyrtsite—'*Vkusat na vremeto*'.
- Toni Dimitrova—'*Za tebe horata govoriat*'.
- Lili Ivanova—'*Detelini*'.
- Emil Dimitrov—'*Moia Strana*'.
- Pasha Hristova—'*Edna Balgarska Roza*'.
- Signal—'*Kasno e*'.
- Signal—'*Sbogom*'.
- Tonika—'Burgaski vecheri'.
- FSB—'*Sled deset godini*'.
- The Brothers Argirovi—'*I zamirisa na more*'.
- Impulse—'*Ako ti si otidesh za mig*' (1984).
- Factor—'*Priateli*'.
- Diana Express—'*Dysha*'.
- Diana Express—'*Ytre*'.
- Rositsa Kirilova—'*Bosa po asfalta*'.
- Orlin Goranov—'*Svetat e za dvama*'.
- Tonika—'*Priateli*'.

- AHAT—'*Cherna ovtsa*'.
- Duet Riton—'*S lubov do kraia*'.

Folk music and dance
- Bulgarian *Pravo Horo*.
- Bulgarian *Rachenitsa*.
- Bulgarian *Kopanitsa*.
- Bulgarian *Dynavsko Horo*.
- Bulgarian *Paidyshko horo*.
- Valia Balkanska—'*Izlel e Delio Haidutin*' (this is the cosmic voyager song).

Stari gradski songs
- '*Yovano, Yovanke*'—is a favourite, even played at my wedding, performed by Tania Sarbinska and Kosta Kolbev.
- '*Hybava si moia goro*'—Georgi Raffailov.
- '*Kaniat me mamo, na tejka svatba*'—The Adjovi Sisters (one of the sisters is my godmother, and a good friend to my late paternal grandmother).

BULGARIAN FILMS
- *The Goat Horn* (*Koziat Rog*, 1972).
- **A Nameless Band (Orkestar bez Ime, 1982).**
- **Tobacco (Tyutyun, 1962).**
- *Doomed Souls* (*Osadeni Dyshi*, 1975).
- **With Children at the Sea (S Detsa na More, 1977).**
- **The Unknown Soldier's Patent Leather Shoes (Lachenite obyvki na neznayniya voin, 1979).**
- *Dangerous Charm* (*Opasen Char*, 1984).
- **The Peach Thief (Kradetsat na Praskovi, 1964).**
- **Ladies' Choice (Dami Kaniat, 1980).**

- *King for a Day* (*Gospodin za Edin Den*, 1983).
- *Time of Violence* (*Vreme Razdelno*, 1989).
- *Khan Asparyh*, (1982).
- *The Last Summer* (*Posledno Liato*, 1974).
- *Where Do We Go From Here?* (*A Sega Nakade*, 1988).
- *The Barrier* (*Barierata*, 1979).
- *Whale* (*Kit*, 1970).
- **Under the Yoke (*Pod Igoto*, 1952).**
- **The Hedgehogs' War (*Voinata na Taralejite*, 1979).**
- **Kaloyan (1963).**
- **Illusion (*Iluzia*, 1980).**
- **Villa Zone (*Vilna Zona*, 1975)**
- **The Queen of Turnovo (*Tarnovskata Tsaritsa*, 1980).**
- **The Gerati Family (*Geratsite*, 1957).**
- *Case 205/1913* (*Delo 205/1913*, 1983).
- *The Boyana Master* (*Boyanskiat Maistor*, 1981).
- *Warden of the Dead* (*Pazachyt na Myrtvite*, 2006).
- *The Three Fools* (*Trimata Glypatsi*, 11 short films released between 1970–1990, animations).
- There is one old Bulgarian classic, from 1963, *Kaloyan*, which may be viewed with English subtitles on the cinema-international.com site. If you scroll all the way down to 'watch free European cinema online with English subtitles', then scroll down to 'by smaller European country' you will find Bulgaria. For the rest, you can either go to YouTube and type in the name of the movie and the full movie will appear, or you can go to bulgarianfilms.com and prepare some Bulgarian food, get some red wine and think how much more adventurous it would be to watch a foreign film without subtitles. I have highlighted some of my favourites.

BULGARIAN LITERATURE (TRANSLATED INTO ENGLISH)

- Ivan Vazov—*Under the Yoke.*
- Aleko Konstantinov—*Bai Ganyo: Incredible tales of a modern Bulgarian.*
- Yordan Yovkov—'The Sin of Ivan Belin' is included in Thomas Mann's 1956 anthology *The Most Beautiful Stories in the World.*
- Stefan Gruev—*Crown of Thorns.*
- Go to www.slovo.bg/old/f/en/index.htm and read Petya Dybarova, Nikola Vaptsarov, Hristo Botev, Chudomir, Ivan Vazov.
- Google Geo Milev, 'September'—translated by Peter Tempest.
- Peter Tempest—*Anthology of Bulgarian Poetry* (600 pages of translated Bulgarian poems).
- Google culture360.asef.org for Yordan Radichkov's short story *Container.*
- Also by Yordan Radichkov in Bulgarian—*The Last Summer* (*Posledno Liato*, 1974), *Gunpowder Primer* (*Baryten Bukvar*, 1969) and children's stories *We, The Sparrows* (*Nie Vrabchetata*) and *The Little Frog's Stories* (*Malki Jabeshki Istorii*).
- Nikola Vaptsarov has 26 poems translated into English at poemhunter.com or Google 'Nikola Vaptsarov poem hunter'.
- Also in 1954, Lawrence and Wishart published a Nikola Vaptsarov volume called *Selected Poems.*
- In the future, I hope you learn Bulgarian and then go on to read all of my favourite authors in Bulgarian—Geo Milev, Nikola Vaptsarov, Ivan Vazov, Aleko Konstantinov, Petko Slaveikov, Pencho Slaveikov, Yordan Radichkov, Yordann Yovkov, Valery Petrov, Nikolai Haitov, Payo Yavorov, Dimcho Debelianov, Petya Dybarova, Stefan Tsanev, Nedyalko Yordanov, and everyone I listed in the chapter on Bulgarian literature.

VISUAL DIARY WEBSITES

Google 'images of Bulgaria' and that will get you started.

For more historical photos that inform you of not only Bulgarian history but also give a glimpse of Bulgarian culture through the decades, go to **www.lostbulgaria.com**. The photos begin with the period of the Russo–Turkish war in 1877–1878, right up to 2000, but note: Bulgaria's communist era begins in 1946 and continues until 1989.

- On Facebook check 'Made in Bulgaria', 'People of Sofia', 'The Magic of Bulgaria' and 'Retro Museum (Automotive)',
- Google 'Bulgarian Photo Gallery by Nikola Gruev' at pbase. com.
- On Facebook check 'Vladimir Gergov Photography' for photos of Bulgarian nature.

BULGARIAN FOOD ON THE INTERNET

- www.findbgfood.com/bgmeals.htm.
- *The Bulgarian Cookbook* by Ivailo Piskov.
- *Traditional Bulgarian Cooking* by Atanas Slavov.

ACKNOWLEDGMENTS

First and foremost I thank my family, the family I was born into and the family I have been fortunate enough to create. Thank you to Baba Danka, Stoyanka and Trifon Yorgovi, Yulia Yorgova Ford, Georgi Marinov, Radka and Todor Stefanovi, Plamen, Nikolai, Todor and Yoneta Stefanovi, and of course my parents Katia and Valery Stefanovi (thank you also for being wonderful grandparents). You have made me who I am today and you have provided much of the material that comprises the story of my Bulgarian life. Thank you to my husband Carrick Ryan, and my sons, Michael (Michail in Bulgarian), George (Georgi in Bulgarian) and William (well, he has a Bulgarian middle name, Alexander), I could not be luckier or happier to share my life journey with you and I look forward to the many more Bulgarian-Australian memories we will create together. I thank my mother-in-law, Gaye Ryan and my father-in-law John Ryan, who make fantastic grandparents to my sons and who coincidentally love Bulgaria and visit even when I am not there. I also thank the rest of my Australian family, my sister-in-law Kara and brothers-in-law, Chris and Heath who I can imagine feel very fortunate to have me as a sister-in-law (this may sound like a joke because I have an innate sense of humour but it is actually true). Childhood friends are considered extended family in Bulgaria and I treasure all of my now life-long friends, Ivan, Maria, Joro, Lubo, Faitsa, Sofia, Ogi and Vladdy. Thank you to all of my Australian friends, you have enriched and broadened my life experience and you make up the Australian in my Bulgarian-Australian life story, Louisa, Michael, Trish, Kirsty, Fiona, Rebecca, Clair, Alea and of course The Other Regina. I thank my editor Kirsty Hine not only for her many hours of reading and re-reading my work but also for accepting my occasionally odd sentence structure, because she knows that is just how I converse. Thank you to my graphic designer, Melanie Atlan for translating my ideas (communicated to her in the form of photos, hand written notes, and long stretched out explanations) into a book cover. I thank my publisher, Amanda Greenslade and her team at Greenslade Creations, particularly Sharnai and Lynne for their generous guidance throughout the entire process of converting a manuscript into a published book and a reality. And finally thank you to Bulgaria, my country of birth and my spiritual home, this book is for you.